Dreams
of a
Loner

Dreams of a Loner

NINA BECCA ANTONIO

Library of Congress Control Number: 2019910355
ISBN: Hardcover   978-1-7960-4811-7
                   Softcover   978-1-7960-4812-4
                   eBook   978-1-7960-4815-5

Print information available on the last page.

Rev. date: 07/24/2019

To order additional copies of this book, contact:
Xlibris
1-888-795-4274
www.Xlibris.com
Orders@Xlibris.com
799185

CONTENTS

Memories of
Childhood Lost

I was born in Crete in the autumn of 1956 on the same day that three female members of the Algerian National Liberation Front carried out a series of bombings on European civilians. It was almost as though that tone would carry on throughout my life. I was the firstborn child of Voula and John. We were a low-income household, with my mother working as a seamstress prior to my birth and my father working as a mechanic. It was a different era. Premarital sex was still frowned upon, and my grandparents were opposed to their marriage. My parents eloped in 1954.

After the birth of my sister May, my mother decided we should immigrate to Canada to be closer to her brothers, Mike and Paul. They were a large, close-knit family, and my mother wanted us to have better opportunities and to be raised surrounded by family. We left Crete spring of 1959 onboard the majestic *Queen Victoria* ocean liner, set sail for Nova Scotia, and arrived in the summer of 1959. My father found employment in a local school as a janitor in Montreal and my mother in a factory sewing furs.

I cannot recall too much about our first years in Canada other than when we lived in what could best be described as tenement housing, which I now refer to as the slums. There were three families living in our house, and each took turns to use the amenities and the kitchen— and these were hotly contested commodities, with my father being the most hotheaded of them all. I can recall him getting violent when he felt another family was taking too long to cook their evening meal.

The building was infested with rats and cockroaches and offered little by way of privacy. Once, when I was smaller, I slid myself under a bed and nodded off to sleep. There was mass panic when my absence was noticed; my mother feared I had wandered out of the house. My father found me curled up asleep, dragged me out by the legs, and slammed my tiny body into the floor. If not for my uncle Paul physically stopping him, I am sure he would have killed me. While my parents both worked, they took us to a lady who took care of children; she was friends of the family. She rarely fed us, and she put us to sleep on the floor. I do not know how my parents found out and took us away from her.

My sister Andy was born in 1961, and the following year, my paternal grandmother left Greece to join us in Canada as my mother found employment and worked long hours in a factory and needed help raising us three girls. Prior to her arrival, Aunt Mary, my mother's sister, looked after us. Where Aunt Mary pampered and showered us with love, our grandmother was firm. My mother treated me and my sister May like princesses and bought us beautiful dresses, purses, shoes, and hats. People often remarked on how well presented we looked. My grandmother treated my mother poorly and thought she was too soft with her parenting. Grandmother would interfere with my parents' marriage and would run to tell my father gossip at the end of each day. This often resulted in my mother being physically abused by my father. I saw the evidence of the beatings on her body. When I was twelve years old, I had an interest in what my father fixed at home, so I joined in.

When he was not home, I would try to fix things. When I failed by the time he came home, I would get a beating. Then he would curse me and say that I should be dead. I was verbally and mentally abused. My mom would come to my room to comfort me.

When my grandmother didn't get her own way, she would hit herself in an attempt to manipulate those around her. When she was much younger and still lived in Crete, she married a Turkish refugee. The Cretan government gifted them with a parcel of land and a house. Together, they started a small market stall, but it wasn't profitable because Grandmother kept giving food away to her family members. Grandmother became pregnant with her first son, John, my father; then after two years, she became pregnant with my uncle Nick. But my grandfather died when my uncle was a baby. As time went by, my grandmother met a forest ranger; they fell in love, and my grandmother got pregnant. He told my grandmother to give over all her land so he would marry her, but Grandmother did not. She was a strong lady. My uncle Bill was born in 1943. She was a social pariah. When Bill was old enough to go to school, he too was treated poorly—even by his half brother, my father. Only Uncle Nick watched out for Bill. My father left Crete to join the navy as soon as he could at age sixteen. During his time in the navy, he suffered a back injury; and while he was courting my mother, he had surgery to attempt to fix the damage.

Sometime in 1964, my maternal grandmother also came to stay with us. The two grandmothers had a volatile relationship and could rarely be left alone in the presence of each other.

I have fond memories of playing with my maternal cousins. We ran, played tag, and jumped on beds—all those childhood games filled with the innocence of youth. When my sister May turned seven, things changed. May contracted polio. In the early '60s, Canada was still experiencing outbreaks of polio despite the introduction of a vaccination program. Uncle Mike took May to the hospital, and when she finally returned home, she was paralyzed from the waist down.

Uncle Mike spent all the time he could spare with May and helped her little body to do physical therapy to avoid muscle wastage and encourage return of limb movement. I remember the compassion in his voice as he praised her small achievements. The impact of May's illness was felt throughout the entire family. Even my father showed concern. I spent countless hours crying because I missed being with my best friend, and when I was allowed to spend time with her, I would bite my nails until they bled.

As May continued to improve, little Andy was growing mischievous, possibly in part due to the fact that the adults were concerned with helping May to recover while Andy was left to her own devices. We were expected to be seen and not heard. Young Andy struggled with this. My grandmother would punish Aby by whipping her with a broomstick until she fainted. I would flick water on Andy's face until she woke from her faint. Now deep down, I think they did not want Andy.

Uncle Bill came to Montreal in 1964. He was so good, and we just loved him. He would try to show us love and would spoil us when he could. He was a truck driver, so he was often away from home for days at a time. But whenever he would return, he would wake us up to read us stories and play with us. He was my father's brother, but they were very different in nature.

Every Sunday, we would go to Mount Royal Park for a picnic. My mother's side of the family, including my cousins, would join us. My father would take us down to feed the swans and, of course, chase them. I guess, looking back, life was still okay then—or at the very least, on the surface, things looked okay. In 1965, my mother gave birth to another sister, Cay. Cay was born prematurely at seven months' gestation. She was a long, skinny red baby; and at nine years old, I declared her mine.

Whenever I wasn't at school, I fed her, changed her diapers, and rocked her to sleep. When she took her first faltering steps, it was I who hovered nearby, ready to catch her. I loved her and protected her fiercely.

Once, when my father was laid up in bed with his back injury, Baby and Cay were playing outside on the balcony. Somehow, Cay toppled over the rail and fell from the third floor to the ground. She always wore a cross on a chain around her neck. How she missed being impaled on the fence below was a miracle. She survived with little lasting damage. Cay was always our miracle. When Cay was around four years old, the other children would not play with her and would sometimes hit her. She always ran to me for comfort, and I would sing Herman's Hermits's song "There's a Kind of Hush."

> There's a kind of hush all over the world tonight
> All over the world people just like us are fallin' in love
> Yeah, they're fallin' in love (hush)
> They're fallin' in love (hush)

Oh, I loved that child like she was my own. Aunt Mary was betrothed to a man living in Greece. Shortly before she was due to travel to Greece to be married, she was hit by a car and was left with an obvious limp when she walked. When she finally arrived in Greece, her fiancé rejected her. Aunt Mary sent a letter to my mother, who was devastated for my aunt. Aunt Mary did end up finding someone who loved her enough to overlook her limp. Uncle Tony and Aunt Mary were like chalk and cheese—Uncle Tony was short and very thin, whereas Aunt Mary was tall and had a solid build.

In those days, teachers were still respected. I never could look my teachers in the eye, but they taught me manners, reading, and writing. My cousins, my sister May, and I all attended the same school. There was a guy named Mike at school. I had a crush on him all my life, but I was too shy to ever let him know. Our fathers had a small grocery store together. One day, Mike dared me to throw pepper at our deliveryman. We were skipping rope at the time, so we maneuvered the rope closer toward him, and I threw the pepper. Unfortunately, instead of just making him sneeze and us giggle, it went into his eyes, which caused a terrible scene. Mike and I got into a lot of trouble, and we heard about it every day until the deliveryman recovered. Also, we had to apologize to him.

When we go to church during Easter, May and I would tell the boys who tried to flirt with us where we would meet them, then we would sneak home and spy on them through our window while we laughed at them for waiting for us.

When school let out for the day, we would all go home together. If Uncle Bill was home, he would take us out to the Canadian Aboriginal reservation to see the tepees. Despite never learning how to swim, Uncle Bill would row us across the lake in a canoe. We would regularly have sleepovers with our cousins, and they never chastised Aby or myself for our habit of wetting the bed. It was simply cleaned up and forgotten about. Life was always fun when Uncle Bill was around. He let us be kids. He was our champion—our protector.

Uncle Bill always did his best to protect my mother from the beatings my father regularly dished out, and it wasn't only my mother who was subjected to regular abuse. In 1968, my paternal grandmother passed away. By this stage, Uncle Bill was living a couple of hours away, and my father phoned to tell him the news. I was already a nervous child and was prone to biting my nails when I was anxious. I must have chewed them too loudly while waiting for Uncle Bill to arrive because the next minute, my father reached over and slapped me.

In 1967, Uncle Bill married a beautiful young eighteen-year-old woman. While they were courting, she would jump-rope with us. Her brother, Paul, had a Vespa, and he would take us for rides on the back of it. I loved the feeling of freedom as we zipped around the streets of Montreal. I felt as light as a bird.

Once, my new Aunt entrusted May and me to go to the cleaner on her behalf. We were so proud to be treated like young adults until we got lost while trying to return to her house. It took us hours of wandering before we decided to hitchhike home. When Auntie found out about our adventure, she took a piece out of our behinds.

My mother was always a house-proud woman. Despite working long hours each day, at night, she worked equally as hard. She painted our entire house every year in the summer to keep it looking well maintained. I remember the time when my father passed out in the bathtub and my uncle had to break down the door to make sure he was okay. I think he was feeling pressured over an affair he was having. We were staying with our cousins at the time, and they brought us to the house to see him. He sent me out to buy him cigarettes, beer, and bread. When I was young, I did not think he ever went to the corner store.

In 1968, my mother took me to Greece for three months. My father had developed philandering ways and had a string of affairs, including one with our school's English teacher. I thought we were just going for a vacation to let her work through their marital problems. In Greece, I got to meet my uncle Nick and his family for the first time. Uncle Nick had five children and was expecting another one shortly. My cousins, on finding out I didn't know how to swim, spent the next three months teaching me. I later found out that our trip to Greece had another reason. My mother went to Greece to procure an abortion. My uncle took me aside and gently explained that my mother was in the hospital and also told me the reason why. The baby was a boy. This was not the first time my mother had an abortion. In Montreal, a Canadian Aboriginal came to our house and performed an abortion on my mother. My grandmother collected the tiny boy's body on a plate and showed it to us after school.

We rarely got to spend time alone with our mother, so one weekend, when my father left to go hunting, we gave Mom a cigarette and taught her how to have a drag. We laughed when she choked on the smoke. Mom's hair was a raven-black color, and we begged her to let us dye her hair blond. It was such a shock when we were finished. She looked so different.

When I approached puberty and my body became more womanly, my father asked me to come into a room with him and lock the door. I did as I was told. Father asked me to come and sit on his lap. When I did, he shifted one hand underneath me and began to rub my bottom. He used his other hand to squeeze my breasts. I tried to push him away and asked him to stop; he refused. When he was finished, he told me not to tell anyone what had happened. From that moment on, I wasn't just scared of my father but also terrified. I did my best to never be alone with him. At that point in time, he was working as a security guard. May was twelve when he started doing the same to her. When my menstrual cycle finally started, my mother silently showed me how to clean up after myself. When the time came for my younger sisters, it was I who sat them down and explained what was happening.

May and I started spending more and more time together to avoid being alone with him. One night while we were sleeping, he came into the room and began to lick my back. I woke up and pushed him away. I slept until noon the next day. Every Sunday, he did the cooking. I sat at the table scared and depressed. He whispered slowly that I had to learn all this. I prayed for the curse to end. I was too scared to tell my mother and sisters issues to cry every time, and when things were bad, I prayed for God to take me. I could not deal with myself and the shame I felt, and still, when it came to mind, I'd feel so dirty.

I met a Canadian boy at church, and I asked my father if I could bring him to the house as a friend to get to know him better. At the time, my father was lying on his bed. He grabbed my head and forced his tongue into my mouth. He told me to arrange a meeting with the boy at Jerry Park. May and I set off to meet with George. We didn't realize my father was following us. He grabbed George by the throat, dragged him to the local cemetery, and told him he would bury him there if he ever spoke another word to me.

Every Friday night, my parents would go out to the nightclub and come home very late. They did Greek dancing. Occasionally, they would take me along. I hated it. By the end of the night, the men would all be drunk and would want to fight, including my father, who was always up for a fistfight. We would catch the bus home, and the driver would always sing songs for us. I liked the bus ride home.

When my grandmother died, May and I had to grow up fast and learn to do laundry and cooking because our mother was working a lot. Our mother had to travel three hours each way to go to work since our father would never drive her. It was a long walk to the downtown district in the summer, but the buses and the metro ran on a regular schedule and came by every fifteen minutes. Winter, though, was bad for everyone. May and I would walk to school. Sometimes, the snow would be at hip level. The school was always well heated, so we never missed a day no matter how cold the walk was. May, at eleven, was washing clothes by hand; we didn't have a washing machine at that time. At thirteen, I was responsible for the preparation and cooking of all the meals. May and I would go to the grocery store for our mother. There was something wrong with me at the time. I would cough nonstop and would have to stop and sit on the stairs until I regained my breath.

Despite all the extra chores we had, our extended family still made sure we had time for fun. Uncle Bill and his wife now had four children, and we all got along well. And they would often have us stay over to play with the children. My father's Uncle Manuel and his wife, Ginia, also had three children—two of whom were intellectually and physically disabled. Their names were Tas, Cathy, and James. James was surprisingly strong for his size, had sharp teeth, and would attack anyone who came close to him by biting them and drawing blood. Cathy would only ever attack Uncle Manuel. More than once, I heard my uncle accuse my aunt of providing him with sick children, like it was her fault. My mother's brother also lived nearby, and we would get to go and stay at his house too. My uncle was like a teddy bear. I loved him a lot.

My father sold the house he and my mother had by the ocean in Crete and used the money to buy a house in Pierrefonds, Quebec. It was a long way from the city, and the small population was mostly of Jewish and Lebanese heritage. Our neighbors were good people; they helped us when they could. Despite this, we felt isolated in the beginning, and we missed our regular Sunday outings to church. My mother always sewed our clothes; we may have been poor, but we were always well-dressed, thanks to her seamstress skills.

Our house was nice. It was a three-story house with a very big back garden, and all four of us would play and—as sisters—yes, we would fight and sulk at the stairs of the house and watch the others play. We had all the great music of the '60s: Tom Jones, Elvis, the Beatles, Herman's Hermits, and many more. When my mom would put on the Greek radio station, we would turn it off. We did not want to listen to Greek music and voices.

Pierrefonds was developing, and we were making friends with a lot of people. My father would take me to the Royal Bank, so as a teen, I had wanted to work at a bank. I was always barefoot. I loved being barefoot. I'm sixty-three at the time of writing this memoir, and

I still love being barefoot. It gives me a sense of freedom—a spiritual grounding. Pierrefonds had a lot of greenery and a little river that flowed nearby. I often visited to sit beside it; it gave me a sense of peace. Every Saturday, our mom would take us to Fairview Mall to window-shop, and she would buy us ice cream as a treat. Then we would ride the bus home. It was nice to get away from home and away from him, and it was good for my mom since he was involved with others.

One day, I found May being teased by a gang of girls about her skin. I was already angry about things that were happening at home, and when I saw my sister being victimized, I became so enraged that I beat up the main instigator. It was a brutal fight, and May and the other girls had to break us up. It worked, though; no one ever picked on May again at school, and May became my little shadow. She followed me everywhere.

One summer, May said she had to tell me something—something that made my hair stand on end and my blood run cold. Father was also molesting her. Together, we decided to tell our mother. Our mother instantly dismissed us. She either didn't believe us or was too scared to risk another beating from our father if she confronted him. She left us to face the devil alone. I will always blame myself for not telling May about what he was doing to me earlier; maybe then she wouldn't have gone through the same hell as me.

There was no one we could tell. Father was a well-respected member of the Cretan community, but they only knew what he allowed them to know. None of them knew the true nature of the monster that lived inside him. May and I were hurting from the very core of our souls.

Our younger sisters, Andi and Cay, started Pierrefonds Elementary School and seemed to be okay. They would laugh and play like all siblings do. They were the true joy of my life. Whenever visitors came to the house, we were expected to go to our room and only come out to eat once the guests had left. This would happen at least once a week.

Our schooling was affected because we struggled to pay attention. For me, I was riddled with shame and guilt. I had always done well in most subjects, but I did have my weaknesses like we all do, and I was struggling. He destroyed school for me. There was nowhere I felt safe. That my own father could do this to me made me suspicious of all males.

May and I continued to do our best to protect Andy and Cay. We would help them with their schoolwork and read to them. We tried to give them everything we had missed out on when we were their age. When May and I were younger, we never had toys—not even a doll to play with. Maybe that's why we loved Andy and Cay so much. Each Christmas, we would stay up past midnight, hoping to catch a glimpse of Santa bringing us a gift, but it never happened. When my father would go for his shower, I would sneak into his room and steal money to buy little gifts for Andy and Cay and to buy lunch for us all at school.

We never wanted to go home from school, and it didn't take too long for the school guidance counselor to become suspicious and to call us into his office. We said nothing, but he still called our mother. He, too, was Greek Canadian. My mother convinced him everything was fine at home. I made a friend. Her name was Des. I used to skip school to go to Des's work. I would hang out all day with her and then catch the train back home. I made sure I was home at the right time, so no one suspected anything.

My father enrolled me into a driving school, and one Saturday, when I had finished the driving course, May went to Des's house. We stayed late and went to the city. When we finally arrived home, my father was furious. We told him we were still with the driving instructor. The Greek family living above us heard the commotion and came to see what was going on, which saved us from a beating. In the morning, I went to the driving instructor and begged him to lie for me. He did, but he warned me to never try a stunt like that again. We were lucky that time; the kindness of others saved us. But we couldn't be saved all the time. With the younger girls getting older, life was a ticking bomb waiting to explode. Soon after, Andy started to act strangely. To this day, Andy struggles to remember what he did to her when he locked himself in the garage with her, but she was always screaming when he was finished.

My father found a job for me in a pharmacy in Mount Royal, the center of downtown Montreal. The boss was a nervous wreck who didn't trust anyone. There was another girl working there, and we became good friends. We would eat our lunch together and talk about anything and everything.

My Grandfather's House

In 1979, my father decided to sell my grandfather's old house and the orange orchard that came with it. I had always loved those oranges, so I convinced James to buy Grandfather's house. Surprisingly, he agreed, and we bought the house with no paperwork exchanging hands. It was all done under the table. Well, years down the road, my father decided to sell the orchard and told Ann she could have the house. The house by this stage was well over one hundred years old. It was missing walls, and the floor was in disrepair. It was in really bad shape. I reminded everyone that James and I owned the house and sold it. Ann didn't speak to me for three years. It was all my father's fault. If he'd been up-front and honest, it never would have happened, but he was always trying to make a quick dollar, and he didn't care at whose expense it came. I couldn't get the orchard back. I had to wear that loss; he'd taken the money and left.

Even his own siblings knew not to trust him. Rumor has it that his grandmother spoiled him. I don't know much about what he was like when he was a child, but he had left his homeland relatively young when he joined the navy as a mechanic. I was told he was a good student. My grandfather's house was given to my grandfather by the government. I never met my grandfather; he died shortly after Uncle Nick was born.

My father ignored his brother Bill, who had a different father. Uncle Nick always watched out for Uncle Bill though.

Coming from the navy, my father was a perfectionist. Everything needed to be ironed perfectly; nothing could be out of place. Even in his old age, he was a perfectionist and would be verbally and physically abusive if he felt things were out of order. My mother was always a lady even when she was a young lass. She was sent off to feed the army and sneak private papers to them. She was evidently well loved and spoiled by her older brother Mike. She only ever received a second grade education but was a skilled seamstress. I never understood why she wanted to leave Greece to sew clothes for others, but it appeared to give her pleasure. My mother's other brother Paul was a guerrilla, and he lived high up in the mountains. My grandmother would send him up food regularly.

All the Pretty Horses

When I was a little girl, we would pass by a place where there were horses. I loved looking at them, and I always wished I could ride a horse, but I was never allowed. Here in Stettler, there is an equine farm with horses and other animals where the lady owner agreed to teach me how to ride. Now I was not very tall, but I did manage to go on top of the horse, and she started to go around the field with me. She was holding the reins for about half an hour, then she let go and gave them to me. I took the reins and slowly went around the field, which was kind of scary for the first time, so the rest of the time was slow. The next week, I took Kathy and George with me. Kathy stayed on, but George said he did not like it, but now he regrets not knowing how to ride a horse. Kathy did well; she could ride. She fell off the horse once, but Beth made her jump right back on. After James' health issue, I had a lot of people come to visit from Greece, including my sister Mary and her daughter Ioanna and my sister-in-law Poppy and her daughter Athena. I took them all horseback riding. Athena loved it and became quite an advanced rider.

Dobbing Debbie
and Donkey Milk

When I was a baby, I had a tendency toward biting, and my mother had to warn other mothers and children not to let their guards down because I would know when they had and would latch on. All the kids in the neighborhood were scared of me and didn't want to play with me unless they were told they had to.

I also liked to tell tales. If Uncle Nick kissed Auntie Soula, I'd run to tell my mum. No secret was safe when I was around. Uncle Nick thought it was hilarious and would regularly set about trying to make me tattle.

I was very sick as a baby. I had an infection in my intestines and couldn't process regular milk. My mother had to feed me donkey milk as it was the closest to human milk in terms of nutrients. It was a painful illness, and I cried often. My father couldn't stand the sound of my cries and once slapped my cheek so hard that my skin was red for quite some time after. My aunt Mary took me to stay with her until I recovered from my infection.

James

D es introduced me to James in May of 1974. I had seen him around before that, James took me to the botanical garden on our first date and then, later, to the top of Mount Royal. He was very sweet. All these years later, I still remember him saying, "Any man who would hit a woman should go to the top of a mountain and fall off the side." We spent the entire day together. It was lovely. He was very calm.

We started to see each other regularly. He would pick me up from the pharmacy where I was working, and May and I would stay at an uncle's house so we didn't have to spend money on bus fares. My father would pick us up at the end of the week, and we would hand over both our paychecks to him. May was working full-time now; our father forced her to leave school to contribute to the household income—a decision that bothered me greatly. I didn't mind sacrificing my own education to help my sister, but I was upset that May was being forced to. When I found out, I told May not to quit school.

Now that I was going out with James, things were a little easier. I was still living with my uncle and only seeing my father occasionally, and he was treating me more nicely. But I never felt at ease no matter how hard I tried. My father didn't know about James. In August that year, my uncle found out and let my father know. My father lost his temper. Our upstairs neighbor, Nick, who knew some of what had gone on in our house, came down, calmed my father, and arranged for him to meet James. Nick and James came to the pharmacy to let me know they were meeting my father. James was going to ask my father for permission to marry me. My father refused.

James turned up at the pharmacy to tell me what had happened, and I told James he should leave. That Saturday, he showed up again, this time with a ring. When word caught on that James had bought me a ring and proposed marriage, the rumor mill went into overdrive. People were claiming that he had a child. I asked him, and he denied it. I was naive, and I believed him. Also, in the back of my mind, I knew James was my way out of the hell I was living at home. We celebrated our engagement by feasting with the people living upstairs.

James had two brothers, Stalio and Larry. I was waiting for James to come and pick me up when two men came in looking to buy diapers. As I walked them to the diaper section, one of them made a joke. I giggled and turned to walk back to the counter when one of them said, "Wait, I'm your brother-in-law Larry, James's younger brother. And this is your cousin-in-law." From that moment on, we became fast friends, and if James was unable to pick me up from work, Larry would make sure I arrived home safely. For the first time in my life, I felt truly happy. James would take me to restaurants and spoil me. He even bought me a beautiful cake on my birthday. Our five-month courtship was a taste of heaven. We would travel to Ottawa with friends. Once, we took May with us, and she met a lovely boy named Mike. May began coming with us every time we went to Ottawa to meet up with Mike. Mike was also from Crete, but he was here illegally after jumping from a ship. May was so happy. We kept her relationship with Mike a secret from our family, but eventually, a friend of the family found out and told my father. The house imploded. Our father refused to allow May to continue seeing Mike, but everyone else could see how happy May was and pushed back. Finally, he calmed down and agreed that Mike could come to the house and meet with him. Mike was a smooth talker and won over my father, and he gave his blessing for May to date Mike.

Now that James and Mike were spending more time at our house, our father stopped being physically abusive to our mother. Like most bullies, he was a coward on the inside, but he continued to have a string of affairs right up until he was too sick to physically conduct them.

In October 1974, Mike asked May to marry him. Life was wonderful. Each weekend, either May and I would travel to Ottawa or Mike and James would come home. I would babysit James's nieces for Soula to give her a chance to rest.

We were married in January 1975. May and I chose to have a double wedding to save on costs; we held the party at the Cretan Association hall. It comfortably held two hundred guests. When we went to the hairdresser, I let the others go first. By the time my hair was finished, the roads were so bad that when we finally arrived back home, my father was cursing up a streak. We put our gowns on as quickly as we could and headed to the church. Father walked me down the aisle, and Uncle Paul walked down with May. We were an hour late, and the guests had been amusing themselves by making fun of the grooms while they waited.

It was a traditional Greek service, and my Greek was never perfect. The priest offered to do the ceremony in English, but I didn't want to rock the boat any further. Following the ceremony, we went to the hall to dance and share a meal with our guests. It was a great time. We'd never been taught Greek dancing, so when they insisted that we join in, we were grateful for the long dresses we wore.

I finally met my mother-in-law, Anastasia, five days before the wedding. She traveled over from Greece. She was a very nice lady, and we got along well. The day before the wedding, James took me to his house, and I met his other sister Thena. Thena was a straight talker. If something bothered her, she wasn't backward with coming forward. Although my parents and grandparents all spoke Greek, I wasn't as confident speaking it as I was with English or French; and with all the drama leading up to the wedding, I was feeling a little reserved. Thena asked me a question while she was washing the dishes, and I didn't reply in a timely enough manner. Thena abruptly asked the rest of the family if I knew how to speak. I was very intimidated by her. James's family spoke with high-pitched voices; to this day, when I hear a high-pitched voice, I get a shudder run through my body. The evening of the wedding, we headed home, and I prepared for our first night together. It was not what I had hoped for. There was no tenderness, no whispered I love yous, and no sweet nothings. It hurt, and even all these years later, I can't forget it.

It wasn't too long before May got pregnant, and a few weeks after that, I, too, was pregnant. It was nice to have my sister, my best friend, on this journey with me. In the beginning of my pregnancy, sex was not something I enjoyed, and I did my best to avoid it. James called me frigid. The men would take off and leave us at home while they traveled for three hours to go gambling. One afternoon, May was feeling poorly and had no money to see a doctor. Worried for her and her baby, I used some of our savings to take her to the hospital. It was nothing serious, and she was soon discharged. I called the men up and had a fight over the phone with James. I told him and Mike how irresponsible they were for gambling while they had pregnant wives at home, and I told him to get home that instant. He didn't reply, so I hung the phone up and called my father to ask if May and I could come home. My father said, "You made your bed. Now you can both lie in them."

James was gambling more often and was inviting his friends to our house to gamble in the evening. I remember one day, he demanded I cook for them all. I refused. My mother did not raise me to be spoken to or be treated as a servant. The men packed up and walked off into the night.

Soula gave birth to her son Nick the month James and I got married. Nick was a lovely little baby. He was the first boy in their family, and he was doted on by everyone. James's sister Cindy also got engaged, and her wedding was scheduled to happen in June. Soula planned to have Nick's baptism around the same time because the extended family from Greece would be traveling over for the wedding.

James and I decided we should move in with May and Mike. May and I were both pregnant and could use a little help around the house, and we would both save money with only one house to keep up.

Living with my sister was nice. We always were close. We were two hours from the city when, one day, we received word that my father had doused a towel in alcohol, wrapped it around his hand, and set it on fire. We rushed to take him to the hospital. The hospital trimmed away the damaged skin and performed a skin graft. My father told everyone the skin came from a dog. He was a compulsive liar. When we were young, we used to hear stories that he would tell, and we would find them strange. As we grew older, we realized that he was a compulsive liar, so all four of us sisters do not lie. We'd rather get in trouble than lie.

During my pregnancy, I experienced some blood loss. Anastasia came to stay with me for a while. I was still working in the pharmacy. Bobby, my boss, was hyperactive, and I was a little frightened of him. When James found out I had gone to work, he tore strips off me. I threw his rings in his face. I was so cross. We went to my parent's place for Easter, and his family was there also. When it was time to leave, he wanted me to stay with my mother. My brother-in-law Steve told me, "You have his name now. Do as he says." That should have been my biggest warning of what was to come. At this point, we were not fighting. He wasn't seriously gambling, but he was beginning to manipulate me. Once, he told me that my father had asked us to bring some bread with us. I asked James if he had picked some up, and he said no. I instantly started to shake. I was scared of my father, and James knew that and used that fear to control me.

Motherhood

Mary's baby, Guy, was born in December. Twenty-six days later, my son, also named Guy, made his entrance into the world. My labor was short but intense, and I squeezed my mother's hand throughout the entire ordeal. Little Guy was the image of his father. His face and hands looked just like his father. I instantly fell in love with him. I didn't want the nurses to take him away. They insisted I must rest and took him to the nursery with the other babies. In the morning, I was still feeling dizzy and weak, so the nurses wheeled me so I could get Guy back into my room to be fed. We stayed in the hospital for seven days. For once, James was home when he said he would be and was excited to spend time with his son. We were the perfect little family. A few days later, colic set in. Oh boy, that poor baby suffered. I started giving him chamomile tea, and it eased his colic, and he would then sleep for three hours each time. The first time I tried to put a diaper on him, he peed on me. This was back in the days of cloth diapers—no fancy Pampers back then. All the diapers needed soaking and scrubbing by hand to be hung out and to be sanitized in the sun. It was a lot of additional work, and we already had two babies in our household.

The two Guys were growing like weeds. With only a twenty-six-day age difference, they were often mistaken for twins. During the summer, my Guy woke with a swollen cheek and a fever, which, no matter how much I tried, I couldn't get to go down. I rushed him into the children's hospital, and they admitted him right away. He was in the hospital for a week. I never left his side. They performed a lumbar puncture test where they removed spinal fluid to test for meningitis. At only nineteen years old, I was terrified. The doctor ended up prescribing me Valium to try and settle my nerves. When Guy was released from the hospital, I wanted to go spend some time with my mother. As I was packing our suitcase, May said she didn't want to stay alone and asked Mike if she could go with us. Mike gave his permission, so May began packing.

Our younger sisters were so excited when we both arrived with the babies. They each took a baby and rarely left them alone, and our mother was no better. The boys were very spoiled. Even our father was happy when he returned from work to see us all. We stayed for a week, and our mother let us sleep in every morning. She got up early, changed the diapers, brought the babies to us when they needed feeding, then took them back to their beds once their bellies were filled. When we returned to our husbands, it was a nightmare. Mike was angry that we were gone for a week and began to beat May. He kicked and punched her and pulled her hair. Mike's brother had to step in between them to stop him. Mike yelled at May, called her a whore, and said the baby was not his. I hid in my room with Guy, too scared to come out. I waited until everyone was asleep before I came out to get some water and use the bathroom. The next day, the tension was so thick you could have cut it with a knife. I was still feeling very afraid of Mike. James was getting ready to head to the Cretan Association to play backgammon, and I asked him not to go because I was scared. He told me to stop being silly, and we ended up fighting. I threw a dirty diaper at him in rage. I just wanted my husband to show come consideration and sympathy for what I was feeling. I ended up taking the Valium again. It was better than walking on eggshells.

When our lease was up and the people living in the house above our mother's house moved out, we rented it. Andy and Cay were always upstairs to help us with the two Guys, spoiling them rotten, and our mother was always cooking meals for us.

The Village

I'd always been the Harlequin and Mills & Boon romance believer and thought James was my knight in shining armor, ready to whisk me off to a house with a white picket fence. While we were staying above my parents' house, he started a brainwashing campaign to convince me to go to Crete. After four months, I agreed. Maybe life would be different there.

The very next day, it was in August, Guy and I were on a plane bound for Greece. James was due to follow at a later date. When we got to Athens Airport to make the final leg to Crete, a relative who was on the same flight asked if I would check in his suitcase with my own. I said okay and did so. Then he disappeared, and I missed my plane. I later found out that his suitcase contained guns. I was lucky not to have been caught! I called my in-laws so they wouldn't worry and then called my uncle in Athens and spent the night at his house where my auntie spoiled Guy and me. When we arrived in Crete the next day, my father-in-law, brother-in-law, and George were waiting to collect us. We headed to my sister-in-law Polly's house.

I fell asleep on the journey there, and Polly came out to wake me. It was the first time I'd met her, but she made me feel welcome and right at home. Her husband, Christ, was also very hospitable. They had a daughter, and Polly was already expecting another child. Anastasia cracked a joke when she saw me. She said that I grew shorter. I guess it was the additional weight that I gained through my pregnancy that made it appear so. I had gone from 123 to 200 pounds!

My in-laws' house was old. The floors were made of cement and had cracks running throughout. The doors and windows creaked, and there was no indoor bathroom. You had to use an outhouse with a wooden fence surrounding it for privacy. You bathed outdoors year-round. It was somewhat of a culture shock for me. I guess I'd become a little spoiled living in Canada. Each morning, the house would be washed from top to bottom. I would scrub the walls and floors, and Anastasia would do all the cooking. She also had a knack for growing flowers. She'd go outside each day and water the garden and pluck out weeds. I've never been much of a green thumb, and plants tend to die pretty quickly under my care.

James's sister Cay, back in Montreal, was pregnant, and Anastasia headed off to spend some time helping her. I was left in charge of the house. I swear, when she left, the household grew tenfold. And none of those people would lift a finger to help. All they cared about was drinking moonshine and eating whatever was available to be eaten.

My father-in-law regularly slaughtered pigs, lambs, goats, and chickens, so there was always plenty of meat available. Once, he brought home six piglets for me to raise to be killed. I was terrified of them, but I didn't say anything, I would head down to feed them with my heart pumping, slam the door close, and run home feeling like Goldilocks running from the three bears.

I made the mistake of watching him butcher a pig once. It took me over two months before I would eat meat again. I only ate vegetables and grains. My father-in-law became my prison guard. With James still in Canada, I wasn't allowed to go visit my side of the family. Uncle Nick turned up at my in-laws' house once to see me and was sent home. I cried to be allowed to visit Uncle Nick and his family, but with Anastasia in Canada, there was no one else to look after the house and cook the food. Each morning, I would get up early to tend to Guy and then begin the cleaning and cooking routine. Thank God for James's brother Mike. Mike was the same age as me and was the only person who helped me around the house. He bought me cigarettes and a bathtub for Guy, and each day, he would help bathe Guy. Mike and his father had a strained relationship. Everywhere I went, there was conflict. There was no laundry machine. I had to wash everything by hand, and the kitchen was an aboveground firepit with a large cauldron. If it wasn't for Mike helping me, I wonder if I would have coped at all, cooking for such a large group of people.

I wrote to James. I asked him when he would arrive in Crete or whether I could return to Canada. I felt so isolated with my father-in-law watching my every move, not even allowing me enough freedom to visit my aunt Mary or my own grandmother. Aunt Mary had enough, one afternoon, and confronted my father-in-law. She told him off for keeping me isolated. He was steadfast in his refusal. Until James returned to Crete, I was under his watch. I am certain that my father-in-law only wanted me around because he wanted the land my father gifted me for my wedding.

At least I had Mike and Xia, James's youngest sister, to keep me company. My husband's uncle and his family came to visit. Their two sons were shepherds and were farming the land. James's uncle and aunt had an orchard full of oranges and an olive grove and were rearing pigs.

James finally came to Crete to spend some time with us. Shortly after his arrival, he disappeared. I didn't know where he had gone. Mike was also disappointed and said that since his family was right here, why would he go to the café to play cards? I was hurt when I realized that gambling was more important to James than spending time with his son. I fled to my room in tears.

James's aunt was helping me wash clothes one day when she commented that James never should have married me. I was shocked and asked her why not. Finally, someone was telling me the truth of what I had long suspected. James had another child named Geo with a woman named Tergani. When Tergani came to see my in-laws with her baby, they asked her to leave the baby with them to raise and never return. Tergani left and took her son with her. I asked James once again, and he denied it at first, but he eventually confessed. After, we went out to the pastry shop for coffee and a treat. I smoked a cigarette to relax my nerves.

With James now in town, I was allowed a little more freedom and could go visit with Uncle Nick. There was so much love in their house. Uncle Nick had a six-year-old daughter, Lilian, who could speak English. I used to spend time chatting with her. She was a clever little girl.

The house that James and I were now living in was on the top floor, and we could see the ocean. It was beautiful. I got pregnant, and despite being upset over James's lying and gambling, I decided to keep the baby and hoped that he would change his ways. I was unable to travel back to Canada while I was pregnant because I was prone to severe swelling, so we had to stay in Crete a while longer. Uncle Bill came down with his family to visit, and I begged him to get me out of there. Bill used the duration of my pregnancy to pressure James into letting me go to Florida with his family. James finally agreed that once the baby was born and I was cleared to travel, we could go to Florida.

The months rolled by, and soon, I was in the hospital waiting to deliver my second child. It was a quick delivery. The baby, a girl, was covered in black hair all over her body and had a bump on her head. I thought she was an unfortunate-looking thing and would try and hide her from people. I even asked to be discharged from the hospital a day earlier to avoid seeing people. I named the baby Cat after my little sister. Kat, like Guy, suffered from colic. My mother had traveled to Crete to be with me for the delivery and had brought my nephew Guy with her. May had stayed a little longer with her husband in Canada.

While we were getting ready to leave and head for Florida, I brought Kat into the village to meet my father-in-law since he had not come to the hospital to see her. He played with her for a while and then I said goodbye. As I turned to leave, Anastasia blurted out, "He can't stand you. Someone saw you at the pastry shop smoking." I was shocked. How could seeing me smoke a cigarette make someone hate me? I got over it pretty quickly. I was leaving for Canada and then to Florida and hoped I'd never have to return to Crete.

Florida

Being back in Canada was great. My younger sisters were growing up. Cat was now thirteen, and Andy had turned seventeen. It breaks my heart to imagine what Andy went through when May and her husband had left. At least now I was back; she was safe. Bobby gave me my job back at the pharmacy, and in the time that I'd been gone, the bus service had improved. It was now quicker and easier to get to and from work.

After we'd been back in Canada for a couple of months, James returned from Crete. He wanted to head to Florida first and send for me later. I was not staying behind with my father. I was still terrified of him. I put my foot down and went to Florida at the same time as James.

I loved Florida! The weather was great, people were happy and friendly, and the beaches were wonderful. Uncle Bill's wife, Sally, had a delicatessen, and I would work there on occasion. I learned how to make doughnuts. I would mix the batter, cook them, ice and decorate them, then sell them. Aunt Sally had her license, and we would travel to various flea markets looking for bargains. Andy was staying with us at Bill and Sally's house. Andy was sleeping in the loft and watching Guy and Kat while James and I were working. One time, I came home and went to peek in on the children who were napping. I found Kat with her neck caught between the rails of the crib and the mattress. Thank God I saw her in time and that she was okay.

Little Guy was crying one morning. His cousins came home with treats and didn't share them with him. He put on a brave face and said, "That's okay. My father will bring me one." My heart broke for the dear little boy. James, to his credit, was good at bringing home treats, and now that I was working at a local restaurant, I would also bring home the occasional sweet treat.

My boss at the restaurant was called Alimonos. He was a very nice man, and his family was nice too. They started me off slowly, and as I picked up, they increased my hours. Something in my brain switched when I turned twenty-five. Things made sense. Things changed. And I realized I'd made a mistake with James. I used him as my get-out-of-jail card, so to speak. But I also told him my darkest secrets. May and Andy had never told their husbands anything about their lives with our father, and they were hesitant for me to even write this memoir. But what good is a book if it is not telling the truth? I want the truth exposed. All of it. So working with Alimonos was an eye-opener. I was making lots of tips and good money, I was on friendly terms with everyone, and Alimonos's daughters always dropped me home at the end of each shift.

One evening, they dropped me off late, and I heard a noise out the back. I figured it was just a raccoon, so I wandered over to the back door and pulled the curtain aside for a peek. It wasn't a raccoon. It was a man. I don't know what he was doing or what he wanted. I didn't give him the chance to explain. I called the police, my aunt, and my uncle. My uncle arrived quicker than the police. But by then, the intruder was long gone, and there was no evidence left to identify him. I slept on the couch with the broom nearby and a knife under my pillow. He came back on two other occasions, each time making a getaway. It was at this stage that I was begging James to leave his job because it meant he'd be away for a month at a time and would only be home for four days before leaving again. His boss offered him a hunting gun, so James spent his first night at home camped inside the glass door with the rifle at the ready. But we never found him.

I didn't want to spoil my children, so by the age of three, little Guy knew how to use the vacuum. Kat, however, oh, she was a handful. She would take off wearing nothing but a diaper and a smile. I would have to chase her down, laughing all the while. She was a darling happy girl.

Our time in Florida came to an end when James said something inappropriate about Aunt Sally, and Andy told her about it. I wasn't at home when it happened, and when I got home from work, all hell had broken loose. We packed up and headed back to Canada. Bobby found out I was back and phoned to give me an earful of abuse because I'd left him in the lurch.

Pierrefonds

I n 1980, on a whim, I applied for a job working as a bank cashier. I'd never done anything like it before, and I never expected for my application to be successful. But they called me up for an interview, and I did well and got the job. I was working with some of the girls I'd gone to elementary school with. It was actually really nice. I would get paid each Friday and would rush out to buy a toy for Guy and Kat. I wanted them to have all the things I had gone without. Guy liked to play with dolls; it never bothered me. I didn't see the harm in it. Guy and James went to Greece to see James's family. They were gone for forty days. Kathy was distraught. She loved Guy and slept in his bed every night. They were so close. I did my best to keep her occupied while he was away.

As the years went by, James and I had our ups and downs. He was still gambling, and I still wanted him to stop. Many nights he didn't come home, and I would pace around the house wondering if he had been in an accident and wound up in hospital. So many what ifs crossed my mind. James has always been an insensitive person. He had known me long enough by this stage to know how my mind worked; he just didn't care.

After I started working at the bank, I realized I was pregnant again. I worked throughout my pregnancy. It was a good place to work. We all got along well, and no one acted like they were superior to the others; even the manager was down to earth. The bank was open on Saturdays, and I was scheduled to work. James was in a mood and wouldn't let me leave the house. To this day, I have no idea what was bugging him. Determined to go to work though, I climbed my pregnant self out the window in the kid's room and walked to work. When I returned home, he was gone. My mother was there; she looked after Guy and Kat for me.

I had an appointment for an ultrasound. I took Guy with me. Oh, how excited he was to see the baby on the screen and to learn it was a boy. He was petting and kissing my stomach. Those children brought such joy to my life.

We would go and visit my parents. Guy loved working in the garage with my father's tools. I bought Guy a little wooden tool set so he wouldn't injure himself using the real ones. The first thing Guy did with his little wooden hammer was to hit my father squarely on the head. I did laugh quite a bit on the inside.

My pregnancy was event-free aside from a few bouts of morning sickness. On the evening of July 26, 1981, I headed to the hospital after an uneasy day spent at my mother's. Five hours later, on the twenty-seventh, I was holding a beautiful, healthy little boy in my arms. I named him Jack. He was a happy, smiling baby, and like Guy and Kat, he grew to love his grandfather.

When my babies were younger, I was scared to touch them or bathe them—worried that I would be like my father. It was a nightmare, but I soon realized that my children would never be at risk with me.

Toward the end of 1981, my father found a man for Andy. Andy was not interested and refused the marriage offer. Initially, Father accepted Andy's decision, but he soon started pushing for a marriage and argued that his friends were saying his daughter must not be a virgin; otherwise, she would say yes. My father was always lying. I doubt any of his friends said anything of the sort, but it was enough to compel Andy to agree to go out with Notie. Notie also did not enter legally in Canada, and after a while, my father wanted Andy to leave him, but she refused. This enraged my father, and he would constantly try and cause trouble. My mother would call me to come help calm him down. She was fast becoming a nervous wreck. I told her and Andy to stay at my house. One day, he stormed into my house brandishing a gun around, threatening to kill Notie. He upset everyone in my house. I was tired of living under his thumb. I tried to convince my mother to permanently leave him. An unrepentant Andy and Notie got engaged in the summer and married the following winter.

In 1982, we packed up and moved to Park Extension into a house across the road from Shawn and Soula. James had been asking me to move back to Greece for a while now, but I was determined that I would not return to be treated as I was the last time. I was happy where I was, and whatever feelings I had for James were not enough for me to want to give up what I had. My job and work friends brought me peace. When Guy and Kat came to visit at work, they were spoiled. The Greek Hellenic Trust would send us to lovely restaurants at Christmas. When the doors would close at the end of each day, we would always stay back to share stories and laugh. In the '80s, the bank began installing computers, and I trained a new girl named May. We became lifelong friends. James was still pressuring me to go to Greece. James and his brothers, Mike and Shawn, had some ridiculous idea to open a fancy restaurant. Again, I reminded him of the treatment I had endured the last time I set foot in Greece. He promised he would not allow it to happen again if only I would agree to go. James left for Crete in March, leaving me behind to make preparations.

By this stage, Shawn's wife, Soula, and her friends were drinking moonshine every day. I hated moonshine, but after the first glass, the rest went down easily. Slowly yet surely, I became an alcoholic. My children were still small, and it shames me to tell the truth, but I wasn't a good mother at this point. For six months, my sister Cat would come and stay from Friday to Sunday just to watch the children because I was incapable. I would wake up in the morning, and instead of reaching for a coffee, I would reach for a bottle of moonshine. Even my father was concerned and turned up to take me back to their house in Pierrefonds. There was a party going on upstairs, so we headed up to say goodbye and walked into a food fight. I covered my father in whipped cream.

Being back in Pierrefonds was difficult. I kept needing a drink, but on the other hand, I had Cat there, so I was never alone. Father was working again and wasn't home all the time, so I would wait until Cat was busy with the children and would search the places where I knew my parents hid the alcohol and drink it. I knew it was wrong and that I was hurting myself and my children, but at that point in my life, I had no control over my actions. I remained with my parents for five months. I would have stayed longer, but Anastasia lied and told me that James was no longer going to the café to gamble.

Shortly before I was due to fly to Greece, Uncle Bill and Aunt Stella turned up to lecture me about stopping my drinking. I sent our furniture before I left, and it was coming via cargo ship. Before I boarded the plane, I was told that my father-in-law had been poisoned by chemicals while spraying the olive grove and orange orchard. He wasn't expected to survive; however, the doctor wouldn't give up. My father-in-law eventually recovered and went back to his usual duties of tending to the land and butchering.

One evening, I was in the village with Guy when he suddenly went limp. It was dark, and I went into a panic and screamed for help. James came running out from the café and raced us to the hospital in the city. It was high fever and dehydration that had caused the episode.

A few days later, the husband of James's younger sister caused a public scene by telling everyone the baby she was carrying was not his. My in-laws all headed to Athens to talk to Xia; she agreed to give the baby up for adoption and stayed with her husband. James quickly reverted to his old habits; he was staying out all night gambling at the café. I couldn't sleep one night, and I was so angry that I marched down to the café and started to scream at James. James told everyone to ignore me and that I was a crazy woman. I ran home crying. I was alone and miserable once again. I couldn't go back to the restaurant because I now had little Jack, and it wasn't the kind of environment where you could have a young child.

A New Debbie

S taying with my in-laws was different this time. Anastasia still did the cooking, and I still did the cleaning the same as before. And of course, there was still a never-ending cycle of people in the house. But this time, I had three children to keep me busy. I enrolled Guy and Kat into school. Neither of them knew a word of Greek, so the teacher pulled me aside and told me from now on I was to only speak Greek to them. *Wonderful*, I thought. I myself had only a basic understanding of the language.

School was hard, especially for Guy. I later found out he became a master at changing his grades from a B to an A. By the time I discovered what he was up to, I was too involved in my own troubles to be of much use. The old Debbie was gone. I didn't recognize the person I now was. I had no husband. I had a man who would come and go as he wanted—a man who barely gave me a passing glance. What's the point of looking like a beauty queen when you're surrounded by cracked concrete and chicken crap? Anastasia was crippled, so I had to work extra hard despite having a heart condition. My father-in-law would send me out into the orchard to pick oranges. I would load my wheelbarrow up with four cases and wheel it down to the packing station. During olive season, the only time we were not out harvesting was when it was raining. My sister-in-law Polly worked alongside me. She has been like my own sister for forty-five years, and we've never spoken a bad word about the other, and I also got along well with Chris, her husband. Polly and Chris's four kids and my three were like siblings. They played and worked alongside one another until we left Greece in 1993. During the summer months, the children would just wear pants and play in the dirt. This went on until someone mocked me by calling them gypsies. I had long learned to bottle up my emotions. I kept my face blank, but the children never played in the dirt again.

At night, Anastasia would teach me things. She didn't push me; she just taught with patience and repetition. I learned to love and respect her. Over time, my father-in-law also softened toward me and began to show me love. My continued efforts to show I could work as hard as they could paid off the morning they wanted Anastasia, who was crippled at the shoulder, to kill a chicken. I'd never done it before, but I insisted I would do it. I asked her to show me where to make the cut to avoid the chicken from suffering unnecessarily and held my breath as I did what needed to be done. We removed the giblets, dipped the chicken into a pot of boiling water, and removed it to pluck the feathers.

Later that night, she began to teach me how to crochet. She was always making little clothes for Kat and taught me how to do the same. My father-in-law taught me how to kill and skin rabbits. The old Debbie was gone. The old Debbie would shudder when my father brought game into the house. I think perhaps it was one last attempt to get James to notice me. I learned how to clean pig heads, dress lambs, and burn the hair off an animal. Nothing I did worked on James, but it did bring his parents and me closer together. My father-in-law was now feeding us. He was buying diapers and cans of baby formula. James was useless, and every time I saw him, it resulted in a fight and verbal and mental abuse.

One Easter, I wanted to buy the children Easter gifts and something for myself. I didn't ask for much money, but he claimed he had none to give. He'd gambled it. We had a fight in front of his mother, and I called him bad mannered. Like all mothers, she tried to defend him, but I'd had enough, and years' worth of stories about his bad behavior came spewing out.

I went to visit May and her family. I also visited Uncle Nick and his family—anywhere I could go to try to feel some love. They treated me and the children with love and respect. I wanted the children to see what a positive male role model was. It was only a one-hour commute from where we lived in Crete to where my uncle lived.

My grandmother was still alive in 1982 and lived in Crete, so I would also go and visit her and my uncle Tony, who was drunk from the time he awoke until he passed out. Grandmother and my aunt used to always tell me that my aunt's house would one day be mine. Neither of them could stand Uncle Tony. My grandmother would stand up to Tony and say, "I won't let you kill her." No one could intimidate my grandmother. Uncle Alex also lived nearby; he was a good man. He took good care of his family. My grandmother was a good woman. Although she'd been widowed young, she brought her kids up with respect and love, and her boys didn't seem to suffer for not having a father. My grandmother, God rest her soul, passed away in 1986 and lived to be 105 years old. She was a wonderful woman, and I loved her dearly.

As much as I loved my in-laws, I grew tired of having to rely on them to take care of us. So one afternoon, I sat my father-in-law down and told him we were not his responsibility and that the children and I needed to move out to force James to step up and take care of his own family. My father-in-law agreed, so we found a house in the city, and he helped me move. It was far from perfect. In the back storage room, there were rats bigger than any rat I'd ever seen before, but we'd already handed over two years' worth of rent. There was no TV set, but my father-in-law plumbed in a toilet and a bath for us. Little Jack was now two years old and had a cyst under his arm that needed surgery to drain the infection.

The surgery date was set, and when they wheeled him away, my father-in-law and James were waiting with me until he returned from the theater to the children's ward. My sister and sister-in-law came to make sure we were okay. Jack stayed in the hospital for a week. He was sharing a room with the son of a French woman. I loved having the chance to speak in a language I was more familiar with. I asked if she had baptized her son.

Since we lived in the city, we went to the beach every day during the summer months. I was supplementing our household income doing a cleaning job. One day, while cleaning a house near the beach, I found a scorpion. I got such a fright. I knew how poisonous they were. I made sure the kids knew what to look out for after that.

Our house had three bedrooms, and to get to the bathroom, you had to walk through my room. James's brother and his girlfriend were staying with me for months, and the girlfriend was so lazy. She never lifted a finger to help around the house. I was working at the family restaurant washing dishes, and I would come home late at night to find the house in shambles and the kids unfed. On the occasions when James and I would get amorous, we would do it on the floor wearing as many clothes as we could in case one of them walked in to go to the bathroom. It reminded me of the village again—when one would leave, ten would arrive.

You might ask why I never left. It's simple, really. James hid the passports, and I had no money. He had me by the scruff of my neck.

We stayed at this house for another twelve months or so and then moved to Pachena. Our house in Pachena was nice; it had three bedrooms, a large living area, and a kitchen. Like my own mother, each summer, I would repaint. On the weekends, we would travel back to the village so the kids could play outdoors with their cousins. Pachena was close to the water, and Anastasia would come and stay with us when she was unwell. It was closer to the hospital, so if she was admitted, it was easy for me to travel between my house and the hospital each day to tend to her. Our house in the village had a large tree in the yard that produced a seed that could only be opened by breaking the external shell with a rock. Anastasia still loved to cook, and Polly and I would clean up for her while we chatted about everything. I loved the weekends in the village. It was hard to believe that I once hated it. I remember one evening when we were entertaining guests, I wandered over and saw a delicious shiny olive sitting on the edge of the table. I quickly swiped it up and popped it in my mouth. I'd barely registered the fact that it wasn't an olive before Anastasia was on the floor in tears of laughter and spluttering out *pigeon poop* in Greek. In my haste, I'd eaten pigeon crap. Despite my horror, there was something about seeing Anastasia rolling around in laughter, so soon, I was joining in along with everyone else. The memory still makes me chuckle some forty years later.

Anastasia was very generous to those she loved but very frugal with herself. She only had one good dress and an extra set of undergarments put aside in case of an emergency. She had her daily house clothes though. If we ever tried to spoil her, she would tut no and shake her head and hands, but she was often buying little things for me, like the beautiful blanket she once bought me.

We would light the outside fire, and we would all sit around it. The food always tasted better when cooked outside with the smoky smell of the wood penetrating it. Every summer, young Xia would travel to Crete. She would stay with me during the week in the city, and on the weekend, we would head to the village. Occasionally, we would go and visit Auntie Mary and my grandmother. Nothing much ever changed there. My uncle still drank from sunup till sundown. Although Aunt

Mary was a big, tall woman, she was nowhere near as strong as my own mother, who worked from the early morning until late in the evening, all while dealing with mental and physical abuse. I rarely saw her cry. Once, shortly before I left for Greece, I found her sitting under a tree in tears. My father had finally broken her. I wished my mother had been the type to clobber him over the head with a pan, but she was always gentle—strong yet always gentle. I wanted her to come to Greece with me, but she would not leave Canada.

Auntie Mary

I would still see my sister May and Mike, her husband. Mike had turned out to be a lousy husband. He was a womanizer and a gambler—a drunken layabout. He would come to my house to beg for money when he had lost all his or pissed it up a wall. I always had money and, in hindsight, was too onerous with it. I lost track of how much money I lost over the years as a result of bailing Mike out of trouble.

Mike wasn't the only useless husband. James was a leopard, and we all know a leopard can't change its spots. At night, I would pace from café to café looking for my husband; if he wasn't man enough to tell me the truth, I was going to catch him red-handed. And he never told me the truth.

In 1983, Andy went to Montreal to give birth to her first son, Mike. I am unsure what exactly happened, but something changed within her, and she became a different person. She became physically violent toward our mother when she didn't get her own way. Andy returned to Greece and had nothing to do with the rest of us. Her husband would not let her. He wanted complete control. We all missed her very much, but there was nothing we could do. Now after so many years, we have become sister with lots of love again. Andy was the black sheep of the family whom no one really tried to fix; she went through a lot with my father. We do not know how far he went with Andy because she herself does not remember.

As for May, her life was little different from mine with the exception being that I didn't have to deal with a string of other women. May was always borrowing money from Aunt Mary, and Aunt Mary would sometimes give Andy some. Auntie used to buy sweets for the children. I wouldn't let her buy them for mine, though. I had my own money and could take care of my own kids. When James could, he would take us out to fish restaurants. The kids loved it when we were all together. James and I would have some bitter fights, but afterward, he was the man I wanted to spend the rest of my life with. But he could never keep it up longer than two or three weeks. So I just focused on making sure the kids had a wonderful time during the summer with lots of visits to the beach, which, now that I had a car and had finally learned to drive well enough to not scare everyone else, was much easier.

The restaurant that James and his brothers Mike and Siffee had opened wasn't doing as well as it could have. Siffee was fooling around with women, James was gambling away the profits, and Mike takes off to Madrid two months every year. It was like clowns running the circus. I had to go into the restaurant every night to wash the dishes, or it wouldn't happen.

Back in Canada, Cat finished college. I was so proud of her. She was the first of us to finish school. She was still living at home and working and going out with her friends—everything that May, Andy, and I were unable to do. Cat was lucky; my father never touched her. He was never given the opportunity. With all the men now living in the building and coming and going from the house, he wasn't game to try it. And Cat remained blissfully unaware of what he had done to us. We never told her. She idolized him, and we didn't want to break her heart, but she could see that we despised him.

In Crete, each morning, we would open the doors and windows to air out the house. The blankets and sheets were hung outside in the sun. Greece is such a beautiful country with beaches and mountains. It is a very peaceful environment, and it is easy to close your eyes and listen to the song of the land. I loved the ocean despite not being a strong swimmer. I loved sitting on the shore, lost in thought. It is why I loved taking my children to the beach so often. I wanted them to have this connection with nature. On the island, you can fish in sea orchards for fresh fish well into the night. Nightlife didn't close until eight in the morning. The markets were filled with the latest fashions. I love Cretan nightlife and midnight espressos with a double shot of cream. The tourists were mostly English, American, and Canadian soldiers on their way to Desert Storm. They would stop in at our restaurant, and I made sure they had a meal to remember.

My father needed to have heart surgery in 1984. Cat had to take care of him as my mother was looking after my grandmother who had Alzheimer's. Cat didn't tell us about the surgery until it was already done and he had recovered. She didn't want any of us to feel that we needed to help her. Cat had a curse on her. After she married, her husband was hospitalized a lot; he had a lot of surgeries done to him.

Secrets and Lies

In 1987, Mike—my youngest brother-in-law—met Nat. She was ten years younger than he was and was absolutely beautiful. She could have been a model. He was so happy. He would make me stop washing the dishes to come outside so he could show her off. I was pleased to see him so happy.

As time passed, I began to feel like my entire existence was a lie. The weight of carrying my secret for all those years was becoming harder. I told Aunt Mary. She cursed my father, but nothing could be done—too many years had passed. I was married, and it would have an impact on the lives of May and Andy, and the last thing I wanted was to add more pain to their lives. May was being abused by Mike, and Andy's husband, Notie, came by my house one afternoon to ask for help in trying to control Andy. Andy, who was pregnant with her second baby, was suffering from a hormonal imbalance, which I realized was prelabor. Two days later, Andy gave birth to a daughter—Electra.

Notie had a fishing boat. Every day, he would sell his haul in Chania, a fishing port in Crete. He developed a bad reputation for selling undersized fish that was not of the freshest quality. His business suffered, and people stopped buying from him. Soon there was no money coming into the house. If it were not for Auntie Mary helping them, they would have been on the streets.

In 1985, my parents and Cat moved to Crete. Although I had wanted my mother to move to Crete for a long time, having my father come with her was not what I had wanted. I had supper ready for them, and my father-in-law was dining with us. My father asked what happened to his smiling girl as if he had no idea of the years of suffering he had caused me. My father-in-law, bless him, was worried it was something he had done to upset me.

They stayed at our house until they found a place of their own. Mike and my father hated each other, so they couldn't stay with May. Mike couldn't stand my father's lies and American ways. To be honest, though, putting up with my father was a small price to pay for having my mother and sister around. The kids loved their Auntie Cat, and my mother loved being able to play grandma, cooking, cleaning, and doing the laundry while I was working nights. She even let me sleep in and would get the kids up, feed them, dress them, and get them ready for school. They found a suitable house after a few weeks, much to the distress of the kids.

One night, after returning home from work, I went to kiss the kids goodnight. Jack was missing. I ran to a nearby church screaming. Cat, my sister, was still awake and heard me screaming from her house. She came running out to tell me that Jack was with her. Each night, he would leave his room and run to Cat. He would curl up beside her and fall asleep. Now that I knew where he was and that he was safe, I thought it was best to leave him where he was.

When my mother became unwell and was in the hospital for a week, we decided to send her back to Montreal; Cat and I went with her. I only stayed a short period of time. James phoned to tell me my grandmother had taken a turn for the worse.

James also told me that his ex-girlfriend Tergani had turned up with her son Guy while I was in Montreal. I'd already heard the rumors that she said she would reappear when the boy was sixteen, and it seemed she was true to her word. Of course, she waited until I was out of the country to do so. James said that Guy wasn't interested in seeing him and that he waited outside the restaurant until Tergani had finished speaking with James. At times, I would wonder why we even got married. Why were we in such a hurry? I wish we'd waited longer. I wish I was back in Crete to hold my children.

Grandmother passed away shortly after I returned to Crete. Mom was still too weak to travel. We buried her in Crete, and her children and grandchildren all came to send her off.

While I was at the restaurant one evening, my brother-in-law slipped me an envelope. Inside was a letter and a photograph of Tergani's son. It was obviously James's son. Mike read the letter to me. I understood more than I realized. In the village, Anastasia had a photo of a cute two-year-old. I asked many times who the child was but never received a response. I knew instantly it was the same child. Tergani left her number, so one afternoon, I got the courage to call and talk to him to let him know he had brothers and a sister who wanted to meet him. A few days later, he phoned me back and said he would like to meet. This was in 1987, around the time when Mike and Nat were due to be married. Nat was radiant; her swollen belly was obvious through her dress. It was a perfect wedding.

About a week later, Guy arrived with his mother in tow. I figured Tergani would stay in a motel, but it seemed she had other ideas. Although my body trembled and I wanted to scream at her to be gone, I put aside my discomfort and made her and Guy feel welcomed. When I spoke to James later, he said maybe the boy was scared. I was a little bit shocked, to be honest. I mean, how much do I have to put up with? The in-laws were annoyed with me for letting her stay; my side of the family were also mad that I was making Guy feel welcome. But it wasn't *his* fault; he was as innocent in this as I was.

My father-in-law told me the truth one afternoon. Tergani had known about me from the moment I became engaged to James. She had followed my life from country to country. She knew every detail of my life—things she could only have known through James. That gnawing little seed of doubt that was ever present in my gut began to grow. I couldn't stand to look at James, much more share a bed with him. My in-laws told me to think carefully about allowing her to remain in my house. My children were shocked about their father's deed. They were crying and asking how their father could do this. It took them a long time to recover from their shock.

Mike, Nataly, and Dino

B y February, Nat gave birth to a little boy. Born on the fourteenth, it was only fitting he be named Vale. The family was elated for them both. Sadly, even a baby born on Valentine's Day wasn't enough to keep Mike and Nat together. One night, Mike came home from work and found Nat in bed with Gus. Mike kicked Nat out. I remember Nat telling me one night that she did it because she did not want to end up unhappy like me; as much as it hurt, I could see the truth in the statement. The separation ended up being very acrimonious, with them resorting to physical violence at times in front of Vale.

Nat was a tomboy; she feared nothing. She was equally comfortable riding powerful motorcycles as she was riding horses. She was reckless. One day, she followed Mike home from the village and deliberately rammed her car into his even if she knew her son was in the car at the time. Eventually, Mike felt the only way to keep his son safe from her and to avoid doing something stupid was to flee to Canada.

With Mike gone, I had extra work to be done at the restaurant. I became the first Cretan waitress. I had learned the skill while living in Florida, and it came in handy. Being multilingual also helped as I was able to easily communicate with Greek-, English-, and French-speaking customers from a wide range of countries. And given that the men had somehow managed to run the restaurant into a hole, being able to engage with as many customers as possible could only be an advantage. If only the men gave up their boozing, gambling, and whoring ways, they could have owned three or more properties. Nat had over $6,000 worth of gold and designer clothes and took regular overseas holidays.

We were always busy at the restaurant with a steady stream of soldiers. My sister Cat had a thing for a firefighter who was involved with a married woman. He was always leaving my sister waiting. One night, instead of waiting, we took her out to get something to eat. A man called Jack took one look at Cat and was smitten. Cat was beautiful and tall with elegant bone structure. Cat could wear a hessian sack and look like she was fresh off a catwalk in Milan.

The next day, Jack came to see James and told him he wanted to marry Cat. Cat was not interested. She was waiting for her firefighter to make an honest woman out of her. Eventually, my parents agreed that she should marry Jack. The engagement party was to be held at my mother's house, and my aunt Soula was eager to do the catering. Unfortunately, Cat was still not in agreeance. Aunt Soula gave Cathy an earful of abuse because she was still refusing. Aunt Soula gave hell to the fireman and demanded he should leave. Aunt Soula never backed down. She was strong—easily as strong as most men I knew—and she did not care for mincing words; she spoke her mind freely.

Every summer, my uncle Bill would come to Greece with his family. One night, he came to our house to try and convince Cat to end things with the firefighter and complained that gossip about Cat and the love triangle was being spread all over the island. Cat finally agreed to marry Jack. Jack was from a wealthy family, and the engagement ring he gave Cat was enormous. She wanted repairs to his house made, so he began renovations, which included marble sinks in the bathroom. Cathy got pregnant, so the wedding was moved forward. It was a lovely, fancy wedding with all the family present. Cat was, of course, a stunning bride; even while pregnant, her dress fit beautifully. Cat's new in-laws owned a small hotel, and we were invited to use the swimming pool whenever we wanted. It overlooked the sea and was very relaxing.

When Cat went into labor, she refused to cooperate with the midwife unless I was in the room with her, so I came as quickly as I could and held her hand throughout her entire labor, stopping only to wipe the sweat from her brow or convince her to sip some water. It was one of the most amazing experiences of life, watching my baby sister deliver a beautiful, healthy baby girl. Cat remained in the hospital for a week and then Jack came and took his girls home. My mother stayed with Cat for a few weeks to help her adjust to the nightly feeding routines and allow her a chance to relax.

My parents bought the house next door to mine. While I was delighted to have my mother so close, I was devastated to have my father right next door. As far as I was concerned, he could fall off the planet. I never wanted to see him again, and I was terrified knowing he was around my daughter.

Sometime during 1991, I began to feel chronic pain. My hand felt like a lump of wood. I began taking more and more painkillers on a daily basis in an attempt to find some relief from the pain. By 1992, I needed emergency surgery to remove my gallbladder. A week and a half after the surgery, I was allowed home. I ignored the list of foods I shouldn't eat and soon learned that this was a bad idea. I ended up back in hospital for another week.

Even after following the correct diet, I was still experiencing health issues. I was struggling to climb stairs, my legs were experiencing unusual swelling, and I was constantly short of breath. My mother insisted I should have an appointment with her cardiologist. The next day, he squeezed us in for an appointment and told my mother to go home and start packing a bag for me. I needed to go to Athens immediately. My mitral valve was badly damaged and in need of urgent repair. My mother was devastated. If my father cared, he didn't show it. But in one way, I was happy I was sick, thinking I would hurt him badly and take some kind of revenge for what he had done to us, but there was no emotion. I was so shocked with the news that I locked myself in my daughter's room for three days; they would come and try to wake me, but I was depressed and would not get up. It took the hospital two weeks. They took me to get me ready for surgery. The day I was supposed to have surgery, they canceled it but came after lunch to take me to surgery. They gave me no sedative, and I was all nervous. When the surgery was done, we stayed in Athens for a week. After a week, I felt strong enough to return to the village to see my mother-in-law. She was delighted to see me. I could tell by looking at my father-in-law that something was wrong; he didn't have to say a word.

She worsened in August. I stayed with her every night. She found it hard to settle and would pretend she was up to do some sewing. I would try and gently steer her back to her bed. She would cry, "Why won't you leave me alone? I thought you loved me." It broke my heart.

Anastasia was put into the hospital when she began to refuse food. I was back in the village, cooking one evening, when I had a sudden thought of her and began to cry. Soon after, my father-in-law called to tell me she had passed away. I think Old George was surprised at how I reacted. I don't think any of them realized how important Anastasia was to me. It was the third of September. She was highly religious and wanted to be with her God. I didn't get to attend her funeral; it was only two months after my major heart surgery, and I was still quite weak.

I remained in Crete for another year after Anastasia passed away. There were no more olives and no more oranges. Cat, my sister, and her daughter Cat would visit me often; that little girl was a ball of mischief in everything. She was the apple of her father's eye. Old George still came and visited me in the city each afternoon for coffee and a nap. It always bothered me that after having known me for nearly thirty years, he still wouldn't help himself or open my fridge.

My dear mother always thought I was the good girl—a good luck charm. She would always rub my head for luck, even after I was married with children of my own. I must confess, I wasn't always good. I had a streak for mischief, especially when it involved my mother and Anastasia. Once, when I had them both over for a visit, I spiked their pineapple juice with rum. They drank an entire bottle and were so happy. They wanted more the next night! Of course, I had to oblige. This time, however, I locked them in my kitchen and played a pornographic movie on the television. Anastasia had never seen a porno before; she was so shocked and laughed like a giddy teenager throughout it.

Honesty

I owe it to myself and to my children—in writing this autobiography—to be honest, to be transparent, and to ask for their forgiveness. When James and I would fight, I would take it out on my children. It was never their fault. I wanted so hard to be different from my father, but in some ways, the apple never falls far from the tree. Although I never sexually abused my children, I did spank them. Whenever something went wrong in my life, my children bore the brunt of it. I want you to know that I love you all with all my heart. I have always loved you, and I hope with all my heart that you will forgive me for any pain I caused you.

The restaurant was struggling. James was still gambling more than he could afford. For over five years, I'd been turning up at the café to raise hell and try to get him to stop throwing our money away. I wanted to leave Greece and go back to Canada, but there was no money for the tickets, and I wasn't leaving without my children. It seemed that all the men in our lives were stuck in the 1940s.

James's brother Larry and his girlfriend, Vanna, wanted to go to the café with James and me. I said I'd go but that I wouldn't stay for long. Ha. By the time they were ready to go home, I'd been asleep on the chairs for ages. I never gambled. I hated card games.

When my father developed heart problems, I was the only one who could care for him. Cat's husband wouldn't allow her to leave, and

Andy was not in a position to be able to. I really didn't want to, but I felt obligated to do so, and it got me away from James for a while. Even James seemed keen; he wanted to be able to gamble in peace.

I headed home to Montreal. My father had rented a fully furnished house. I stayed with him. I was constantly scared, but I did what needed to be done. I cooked, cleaned, and washed his clothes. In the evening, I would sit and watch TV with him or talk about world events or newspaper articles. I was always more on edge when the darkness came and would make sure my door was locked. After a few weeks, he was admitted to the hospital for three days' worth of post-op testing. After successful test results, he underwent open-heart surgery. The surgery went well, and he was home within a week. I now had to give him sponge baths at home. It brought up a lot of repressed memories for me. I had to see a counselor. Life goes on, or so she said.

Once my father had recovered enough to care for himself, my brother-in-law gave me tickets to go to Newfoundland. Stee and Soula were living in Saint John's and owned a pizzeria. Larry, Van, and Mike were also there. Mike had been hiding out in Newfoundland since he kidnapped his son Tino and Interpol started looking for him. In the middle of the night, Mike wrapped Tino up and fled from Canada to the States to stay with his sister Thena. It was a risky move, but he avoided detection. Before they left, I spent a week playing with Tino and trying to get him to eat a decent meal. He was a picky eater.

When I headed back to Montreal, Helen had some papers drawn up so I could be paid. I bought all the kids clothes and Canadian treats that were unavailable in Greece. She also encouraged me to go to the Greek Hellenic Trust to see whether I could get my job at the bank back so that everything would be settled if I decided to return permanently in Montreal.

I headed back to Greece and told my brother-in-law Christ that I was taking my children and going home to Canada. I asked Old George if he could build a house for his son; he said no. I told him I was taking my kids and going home. I told him, and I regret it to this day. I could have just taken the kids and had government help to raise them and be free from him. He said we could go anywhere but Montreal. Stupidly, I agreed, and we ended up in Moncton, New Brunswick. The brothers were setting up a new restaurant for us to operate. We lived in a hotel until we found a suitable house to rent. My parents were back living in Montreal; Mom had a stroke and couldn't travel. I took Andy and her children with us. Andy had decided to leave Notie. Montreal was much nicer now; it could no longer be called the slums. A Spanish company had moved in, and it now had Spanish-inspired architecture.

Andy's decision to come along with us meant I had a lot more work on my plate. I helped her find a house, all the furniture they needed, and suitable schools. Andy couldn't handle the time it was taking to sort things out. I think staying in the house with our father was too much for her to bear, so she ended up heading back to Greece. If I could have taken her to Moncton with me, I would have, but the place we were staying and working in belonged to James's family. Andy didn't say goodbye to me. I didn't even know she was gone until I had called my mom to let her know we had found a place for her. There was always a tribe of children around; our nephew Guy and niece Ally were often over playing with our Guy, Kat, and Jack. Mike and Tino were back again, still on the run from Interpol. Even Old George, my father-in-law, came to visit. The house was always full.

The owner of the restaurant we were running was building another restaurant an hour away from Moncton. He wanted Larry to run it. Mike and Tino stayed hidden away at our house with my father-in-law. It was difficult. Tino was upset with Jack for spending time with me.

Cat was due to have another baby shortly and wanted me with her again. On the thirtieth of June 1993, we were in the delivery ward. The doctor was a bit of a smart-ass; he told me to stand at the business end assuming it would be too much for me to handle and that I'd want to leave. No such luck. It was amazing. I was there when my niece Rebe crowned and then drew the rest of the body.

Each evening Guy would rub my Dad's back and in the morning, my Dad would make them French toast and cereal. This was a real treat for them as we had nothing like this in Greece. One day, I took my nieces Cat and Electra and nephews Jack and Mike to La Ronde to ride the amusement rides. As we were packing up to leave, Mike decided it was a good time to start teasing Electra. He was shocked when I pulled rank and put him in his place. We stayed for a few weeks before returning to Moncton. I probably should have stayed in Montreal a little longer because we were not even back in Moncton for a week before James and Guy headed off to Newfoundland to learn the new restaurant menu and left me and the kids alone.

The island of Crete has beautiful forests and rivers and is surrounded by the ocean. It has a wealth of history and is very industrial. The three provinces are filled with olives, oranges, and a wide variety of vegetables. It was bizarre watching the fruits and vegetables die away in the winter and reappear during the spring and summer months in Canada. It was the same with people. Come the winter months, the people disappeared. They headed to Europe where the weather was temperate all year round. The islands surrounding Greece were particularly popular due to the beautiful weather, the architecture, and the history of the city of Athens.

In 1986, when my parents and Cat came to stay in Greece, I used to drive Cat into the village. She was shocked at the environment; she was used to urban and metropolitan environments with high-rise or heavily built-up areas. When she saw my father-in-law butcher an animal, she cried and refused to eat it. We begged her to eat and reminded her that all the meat she had already eaten throughout her life was butchered in a similar fashion. She looked at us as though we were all crazy, although as time passed, she, too, became accustomed to life in the village and began to eat the food grown and prepared locally.

Cathy

W hen I decided to leave Greece and go back to Canada, Cat took it badly. She yelled that she hated me. She hated that I had married her off and was now leaving her alone in a foreign country. It was a guttural cry that wracked and heaved her body. I love all my sisters, I truly do, but Cat was always my baby. It broke my heart to hurt her like this, but of all of us sisters, Cat was the one who had a decent husband—one who provided well for his family and took care of Cat. My family took advantage of the good and generous nature of Cat's husband, Jack. They didn't respect him, only his money.

It took over three months to prepare the Moncton restaurant for business. The first day we opened was hectic. We were so busy; no one had time to show me how to use the new computerized cash register, and I was struggling with the Canadian style of waitressing. We were already busy when a tour bus pulled up. I was near tears. The gentleman who had just finished installing the cash register took pity on me and stayed behind to help me take orders and run them through the machine while giving me a quick lesson here and there. His name was Roudy, and he stayed with me the entire night. I also had two wonderful waitresses, Lnnie and Blossom. They were seasoned waitresses who knew how to take good care of the customers. They glided around the restaurant like they were skating on ice. Lnnie was a native of Newfoundland and had the biggest heart. She was hilarious and kind. I could talk to her about anything. Blossom wasn't as nimble on her feet as Lnnie was, but she sure was a hard worker, and the customers loved her. Together, they were a wonderful team and were wonderful teachers. In no time, I was gliding around the restaurant just like they did.

It seemed that almost each day brought a new tour bus. Business was booming. A funny thing I recalled was the time a lady ordered a Caesar. When I brought her out a Caesar salad, she looked confused. She had wanted a Caesar cocktail—a Canadian alcoholic beverage. I had to learn how to make one, pronto!

Mike, my brother-in-law, was still evading Interpol and turned up to stay with us in Moncton. We had a nice house in a decent area near the restaurant. Moncton was the perfect place to raise kids. Magic Mountain was nearby, and there was a zoo and a water park. Everything you needed was right at your fingertips. There were also some interesting food on offer, like Beaver Tails. I grew quite fond of them in the five years we lived in Moncton. Beavers are plentiful on the lake.

Once, my mom broke both her legs. Always one to bring problems onto myself, I had to help her even though I needed to work long hours at the restaurant, so I invited Mom to come stay with us. My father invited himself along with her. My kids, bless their souls, took care of their grandmother while I was busy with the restaurant. I never got over my fear that my father might molest my children, though, so I was happy when he spent his time away from the house to put all his money through gambling machines.

My kids now tell me that their school experience in Canada wasn't enjoyable. Having lived in Greece for a decade, the Canadian system seemed foreign to them. Guy was now seventeen, Cat was fifteen, and Jack was now eleven. The elder two were quiet and well-behaved. Jack, however, was a handful. My father used to feed into Jack negative behaviors. One time, he convinced Jack that he had killed his own mother with a knife. When Jack was no more than five or six years old and still living in Greece, my father and Jack would go out to the watermelon fields and carve the melons. My father would always blame Jack. He also encouraged Jack to drink moonshine. I would ask him to stop, but it was like talking to a wall. Jack adored my father, and he would only listen to him.

James never raised his voice or his fists to our children, but he also never kept an eye out for them or wanted to spend too much time with them. If we went swimming, he rarely came with us, but like I mentioned earlier, he loved taking us to fish markets. It was the one time you could see true happiness on his face.

The kids began to adapt to living in Canada. Guy was often asked funny questions by the kids in the class at school, like whether they had french fries in Crete and if ladies shaved their armpits and legs in Greece. Where my children were advanced in their education in Greece, by Canadian standards, they were behind, and Guy had to repeat a year due to his English results. It was easier for Cat and Jack, although Jack fell in with a bad group of kids. Due to the long hours I was working, there wasn't as much supervision as there should have been.

The restaurant had a lounge, and men would come to drink. I used to joke they were all happily married until they were drunk, and then I had to listen to all their sob stories. I'd heard all the stories before, so it was a case of in one ear and out the other. But until they decided to pack up and go home, I had to stay open and couldn't close and go home. Then I had to wait for James to come and get me, for despite having had driving lessons, I wasn't comfortable driving in Moncton. I'd go home, shower, fall into bed, sleep, wake up, shower, and repeat.

In addition to tour buses, we became a popular venue for weddings. Weddings were hard work. I had to set the venue with menus, decorate it to the customer's specifications, liaise with the local hotel for accommodation, and set the breakfast and lunch menus as well as the event catering—all while dealing with our regular customers. Since Abbie was the fastest, we put her in charge of venue catering.

At Christmastime, we would host a Christmas party for the staff and housekeeping team. It was a good time. Those who drank too much were able to stay in one of the rooms. My cousin Liana's time in Canada was a culture shock; she couldn't believe how cold it was compared to Greece.

Even after her stroke, my mother had a fast metabolism and could eat whatever she wanted. She practically dared Liana to keep up with her by forcing her to eat breakfast every morning and reminding her that eating when it was cold was a great way to warm your body up.

My mother was always a thankful person. Every time I helped her up the stairs into the bathroom and helped her get ready for her shower, she would bless me. Every single thing I did for her resulted in a blessing from her.

She couldn't navigate the stairs by herself, so we converted a room in the downstairs section of the house for her. Liana was learning to speak English, although it was a slow process. She learned French a little more quickly. Liana started working as a waitress in the restaurant on occasions when we were understaffed, so she had some money of her own. She received tips, and I paid her through the business at the government's award rate.

Interpol

My house was soon overflowing with people. My father-in-law, George, came to stay; so now, in addition to James and our three children, we also had my mother, my father, Liana, Mike, and Tino staying in a three-bedroom home.

One afternoon, a couple came into the restaurant and ordered a drink. They made idle chitchat, which I engaged in without too much thought. They asked whether I knew of a child around seven or eight years of age who could play with their own child. I said no and thought nothing more about it.

That evening, when I returned home, everyone was asleep except for Mike, who was pacing and peeking out behind the curtains. I did the same and saw an unfamiliar vehicle parked on the road outside our house. I thought it was peculiar but wasn't disturbed like Mike was and went to bed. The next morning, I left for work early. Sunday was buffet day, so we started early because it involved a lot of work. I received a phone call alerting me that the police had forced their way into our home and were arresting Mike. I called my brother-in-law Larry who was working in Newfoundland to come home immediately.

The entire house was in disarray. The police were everywhere. They had knocked on the door and convinced little John that they were selling chocolates and pushed their way inside the house. They quickly cuffed Mike and took him to the local holding cell. Tino was placed in a foster home until Nat arrived from Greece to collect him. Other police officers interrogated me and James. James's English was so bad that they needed an interpreter in the room with him, and he would only answer questions with a yes or a no.

They would not tell us where Tino was. The next day, I went to see Mike in jail. It was too much for me to deal with, seeing Mike behind bars and not knowing where little Tino, who was like a son to me, was. I could feel my heart struggling with all the stress. Eventually, they brought Tino in to see us, and we were able to spend one last day with him before Nat took him back to Greece. Tino didn't want to leave his father's side. Mike was deported back to Canada. Mike was lucky Nat forgave him for keeping Tino from her all those years. When Tino saw his mother, he exclaimed, "I have a mother! And she is beautiful." It was sad to see him go, but I was also happy for him; little boys need their mothers.

Life presses on. My father, who was always a very clean person, couldn't stand living in the house with my father-in-law who had a tendency to leave mucus everywhere, so he left to rent a place for him and my mother. Before he left, he said some hurtful things and claimed I cared more for my in-laws than I did my own blood. He completely ignored the fact that for years, I had helped with the care my mother needed and the time he needed nursing after his heart surgery. One evening before they moved out, my father was feeling unwell, and my daughter Kat took him to the hospital, and he screamed at her for no reason. She was still a teenager, and as his granddaughter, she certainly did not deserve the treatment he leveled at her. I could never imagine speaking to any person the way he spoke to her that day, much less my own flesh and blood. I was glad when he moved out.

His words sent me into a deep depression. All I did was work and sleep. I didn't want to get out of bed. My in-laws kept pushing me to get up and put one foot in front of the other. So many times, I wanted to tell them what he had done to me as a child, but I kept my mouth shut. But sometimes, a look in their eyes told me they knew I was keeping something from them.

Debbie

I met Debbie in 1995. She owned the building we rented, and we became close friends. We were together for up to eighteen hours a day, seven days a week. Every day, we would go to the farmers market; on the weekends, we went out for coffee. We found a café that served coffee in soup bowls. For the first time in years, my life was more than just work.

Visa requirements meant that my father and my father-in-law had to spend six months of the year in Canada and six months in Crete. Whenever my father was with us in Canada, he was working on fixing up his car. Jack had turned wild and started hanging out with his friends Lasey, Tod, and Jerry. They used to hang around outside our house and play. As they say, wild attracts wild, so my father was always chasing the kids, usually with a hammer in his hand. Lasey's father was a criminal lawyer, and he taught Jack a lot of legal information. Jack was a smart kid; he was street-smart, but he made a lot of mistakes and got involved with drugs. I found out about his habit when I found his stash when I was doing the laundry one day. I confronted Jack when he came home, and he yelled there was nothing else to do since we were always busy and he was always alone. I told him to stop, but every week, I would find more.

By now, he was a teenager and stood taller and outweighed me by a good few pounds. We had a big fight about his drug use, and he pushed me down the stairs and ran out of the house. The school was calling me every week because he refused to hand in homework and was causing riots on the school grounds. They couldn't control him, and I was at a loss for what to do. James was still gambling, and he didn't come home until three in the morning. My OCD for keeping the house tidy was getting worse. Liana was like me and was also obsessed with cleanliness. We tried our best, but as quickly as we cleaned, the constant stream of men would mess it up again. I was used to it and held my tongue, but Liana tore strips off everyone and told them it was unfair that we were subject to the same mundane chores and disrespect from them day in and day out. Like with most things, it went in one ear and out the other, but I appreciated her effort.

Occasionally, Debbie, Liana, and I would go out for a drink and forget about work for the night. One of the hotel managers, Rus, suggested we should get some of the hotel and restaurant staff to go out with us, so we did. Rus was from Newfoundland; he was a good guy. After we finished at the club, we all went to Rus's room. I didn't want to go; I needed to sleep, so Liana and I headed home to sleep. Cat, one of my waitresses, let one of the waiters drive us home in her car because she had been drinking. As he was driving us home, his girlfriend fell out of the car and landed on her backside along the Trans-Canada Highway. She was okay, but it gave everyone a terrible fright, and she couldn't sit straight for a few weeks. Thank God nothing had been coming in the opposite direction. I can't recall the name of the waiter all these years later, but at the time, he did all my maintenance. I liked and trusted him until I realized that my till was short and that he had taken the money to buy cocaine.

Uncle Nick—the Father I Wanted

In the mid-1980s, Uncle Nick took my father out on his fishing boat. In the middle of the bay, Nick asked my father if he had molested us. Uncle Nick said my father vehemently denied it, and it caused such a rift between them that they no longer spoke to each other. Uncle Nick cared so much for us. I always felt loved by him. When my mom ended up in a hospital in Greece, Uncle Nick came to visit her, and my father kicked him out of the hospital. He tried to communicate by yelling at him, but Uncle Nick never uttered a word to him. I followed Uncle Nick down the stairs and found him crying. He said that my father was as good as dead to him; he means nothing to him. That's the kind of person Uncle Nick was; he was sensitive, but he was strong. And he knew, brother or not, that what our father did to us was unforgivable. Oh, how, when we were younger and even now, we wished that our mother had married Uncle Nick instead of his brother.

Debbie was seeing a man named Rian, and we were friendly with a couple named Jackie and Senator. I can't remember what Senator's real name was, but we called him Senator because his brother was a Canadian senator. We hosted Easter at our house the year after we had bought our own house. Down the side of the house, we set up two of the buffet tables from the restaurant and had a lamb cooking outside, stuffed filo cheeses, potatoes, and rice; we had a large spread of food available. My Canadian guests, except for the Greek families, had never seen lamb before. They all loved it except Debbie, who only ate salad. Debbie was always watching what she ate; even at the restaurant, she was fussy about her food. It was always fun going out to drink with Debbie, but going out to eat was a different matter.

The end of March marked our fifth anniversary of running the hotel. For five years, we had run the hotel at capacity filled with men from different warehouses in the area; after their shift, they would come for a meal and get drunk before finally stumbling home at 3:00 a.m.

October 6, 1995, was the day my heart broke for the second time; my Uncle Nick passed away. Liana was unable to go to the funeral due to immigration red tape. As my father was getting ready to head to Greece for the funeral, I told him that the best brother had died. I don't think I will ever get over losing Uncle Nick. I miss him to this very day.

In the summer of 1996, Uncle Nick's granddaughter, Ellie, came to Canada. Oh boy, that was an interesting saga. Ellie hated English but attended an English school. It was an enormous culture shock. Ellie was also used to being spoiled rotten by Uncle Nick and Aunt Soula. Liana was married at thirteen years of age—yes, thirteen. Her husband was a bully, and he made her life a misery. He would regularly subject her to beatings and cruel punishments as well as financial and psychological abuse. Liana's life was terrible.

The only kids that Ellie felt comfortable communicating with in Canada were my children. They didn't remember Ellie from Greece, but the four of them managed to get along quite well regardless. Just recently, they confessed to me that Kat and Ellie used to sneak out the basement window and go shopping. Jack used to sneak out to hang out with his friends. Kat also brought a bottle of tequila in Mexico on a school excursion, and Ellie and Kat drank the entire bottle, worm and all. I guess my little angels in the basement were little devils after all.

My parents continued to make their six-month visits each year. One year, James's eldest son, Guy, came to stay in Canada for three months. We regularly had him during school vacations when we were living in Greece, so it was nice for the kids to see their brother again. Although when they first found out about him they were upset like I was, at the end of the day, it was never his fault.

As I earlier mentioned, the four kids—Guy, Kat, Jack, and Ellie—struggled to adapt to life in Canada. Having lived most of their lives in Greece, they missed the friends they had made through elementary and high school. They also had more freedom in Greece; the weather was warmer, so they could stay outside and play much longer there. The snow and below-zero temperatures in Canada really bothered them. Although they slowly came to accept the beauty that Canada offered, for Guy and Kat, their hearts belonged to Crete. Jack was Canadian through and through.

James was never much of a communicator. He never complimented me on a new haircut or dress, never told me whether he liked a meal I had prepared, never praised me for doing something well, and never acknowledged all the hard work I put into the home, the restaurant, and the combined families. I doubt he could even tell you the color of my eyes. Our only communications seemed to wind up as a fight. He never had anything positive to say about anyone.

One Christmas, the kids bought him alcoholic drinks in an attempt to try and get him drunk. He was still playing cards constantly. He would even play against his father, George. If James didn't win, he would pitch a fit. By the end of the month, when he had no money left, he was like a bear with a sore paw to everyone. It was never his fault though; someone else was always to blame. When he was at the restaurant, though, it was a different story. He had them all fooled. They thought he was an angel. Those who had been invited into our home, though, saw the real James. Jack's friends were subjected to regular abuse. Jack said this was the reason he started dabbling in drugs. I had begged James to spend time with Jack, but he was too interested in playing cards.

Calgary

W e remained in Moncton for another five years. In 1996, at the hardware warehouse, I met a Frenchman. I was pleased to be able to show off my French-speaking skills, and we began talking and flirting with each other. He came to Moncton for two days each year for the next three years. It never progressed beyond flirting, but it was nice to have someone say nice things to me. I was starting to worry that someone might think it was more than what it was, so when we decided to move to Calgary, I was pleased. Kat, who was now seventeen, was off to college studying tourism in New Brunswick. I arranged for the moving truck and loaded all our possessions. The journey between Moncton and Calgary took the truck three days. Jack, Guy, Liana, Ellie, and I were in the caravan and took turns driving; we made the journey in under a week. We only stopped to eat or to use the restrooms.

In Calgary, my brother-in-law Larry, James and Laki, had a Greek restaurant. My father-in-law, George, was staying with Larry for a while. After we ate, Larry took us to his house in Calgary. It was filthy—truly filthy. We were sorry we had arrived. Liana and I set to work right away to try to clean it up. I did the bathroom, Liana did the living room, and it took a combined effort to do the kitchen. Once it was done, we were exhausted. The next day, we left for Airdrie. I'd always thought I'd grown up in the slums; well, the bar in Airdrie reminded me of an old

Mafia saloon. It was dirty, and you had to think twice before speaking to or looking sideways at people. We were taken to our room—Liana and Ellie were sharing a room, James and I were sharing, and the boys shared a room. I was never able to keep anything from James. I had told him about the Frenchman, so whenever we ran into him, James would make a point of being overly affectionate toward me. The carpet in the room was worn in some places and torn in others. It looked like a junkie's den or a brothel, but there was no other option for the time being.

The next day, we headed to the restaurant we had leased. The owner came to give us a tour. Liana and I took notes. That night, we cried over how much work needed to be done. I don't understand what is so difficult about closing the restaurant for one day twice a year to do major cleaning. The entire restaurant needed cleaning and fumigating: the kitchen, windows, carpets, booths, and tables—everything.

The next morning, Liana and I tied our hair back, put on our oldest clothes and rubber gloves, and began to clean. We cleaned until night fell. After a week, the boss came to check our progress and to see when we would be ready to open. Larry introduced Liana and me as his staff. I was hurt.

Ellie and Jack were enrolled in the local high school. Jack refused to go and wanted to leave school permanently. I allowed him to leave, although it is now one of the biggest regrets of my life.

The restaurant finally opened, and we retained some of the original staff. This turned out to be a terrible idea. My niece Matacy was supposed to start working when we opened, but she was delayed until January. Larry's bartender, Peter, was an alcoholic. His morning coffee was mostly alcohol, and he drank it all day long. He was also partial to knocking back the occasional eight ball of drugs at work. The cook was Fino, another Greek expat. He liked to try and match Petro drink for drink. If you had dropped a match in the kitchen, the fumes from Dino and Petro could have started an explosion.

It didn't take long for Jack to gravitate toward the wrong crowd in Calgary. Where it was weed in Moncton, in Calgary, he became addicted to cocaine. James and I were constantly fighting about Jack. We were renting an apartment with Liana and Ellie. It was hard to find a decent rental at the time, so we took the first one that was available. It wasn't too bad. Guy headed back to Moncton for college, so he didn't lose credit points, and he would come back during each break. When Kat finished college, she came to Airdrie for a visit and told me she was heading back to Greece for good. She was old enough to make her own decisions, and although I was going to miss her terribly, I knew I had to let her live her own life.

The house we rented was across the road from the school where my niece Ltacy enrolled her children Thena and George. I would pick them up from school when Ltacy was working. Ltacy worked the day shift, and Liana and I worked the evenings.

The restaurant wasn't doing as well as we had hoped, and we were often short on wages. Petro was always paid, but the rest of us had to wait. James and Larry were always arguing about Petro, but Larry refused to get rid of him. Ltacy got hooked on gambling too, and she was the type who took her losses out on everyone around her. In the four years we had the restaurant, Ltacy would do half jobs. She would serve tables and take tips but would not return to clean the tables, leaving them for other staff members to do. One day, about two years after she started working for us, she had a fight with Larry, and she walked out halfway through her shift. I was called to come in and cover for her.

Jack, wanting to try and right himself, left Calgary for Moncton to try and get himself off cocaine. One night, I received a call from the police asking about Guy, but Guy was visiting us in Calgary. It turned out Jack and his friends went to the house we owned in Moncton with candles and alcohol and made a hell of a noise, and the neighbors reported it to the police. Luckily, I was on good terms with most of the police officers as they used to come into the restaurant each day for free coffee and breakfast. They told me they had handcuffed him because he was giving them a hard time by running all over the place and making them chase him. They asked if I wanted to talk to him, but he was just howling. I begged him to come home, and five days later, he was back in Airdrie.

Airdrie was an upper-class area. If people liked you, they liked you forever. It had a theater, a mall, a coffee shop, and a bar. Working at the small bar across the road from our restaurant was a Filipina waitress. I had heard reports from a customer that she was very good. I went to speak with her. Lou played a good game of hard to get, but soon she was working for me. She was a hard worker, and there was nothing obvious to make me suspicious. The till was often short, but with all the gambling and drinking that went on, I assumed one of the men was taking it. Lou had an enormous ring; she told me it was diamond. It was the biggest ring I'd ever seen. She told me that back in the Philippines, she was royalty and had a title. None of that mattered to me as long as she did her job well.

One morning, Lou called and said she was in the hospital with breast cancer. We were all terribly shocked except for Liana, who told me she thought it was all a lie. I chastised Liana for saying such a thing about Lou. Liana insisted that I open my eyes and look at the facts—the money only ever went missing when Lou was working.

Three days later, Lou called me and asked me to come to her house. While there, she unbuttoned her blouse and showed me her bandaged chest. I felt dreadful for listening to Liana. All Lou's customers had sent her expensive bouquets of flowers. Liana was still laughing and refusing to believe any of it. The next day, Lou disappeared. We never saw her again. Liana was right. She'd been playing me for a fool all along. I'd rather be considered too trusting than too cynical, though.

The most popular crowd at our upstairs bar was the eighteen- to twenty-five-year-old age group. My nephew Guy worked the bar. Guy was much bigger than my Guy and Jack, but they were all scared of my Jack. Whenever a fight broke out, Larry would have to jump in to break it up. There was a lot of drugs—cocaine and others—going on in the bar and the dining room. Petro and some of the customers were not even discreet about their drug use. Once, while I was using the restroom, one of the customers dropped their stash on the floor, and white powder spread everywhere. When I complained to Larry, he just shrugged and told me to mop it up.

As One Returns, Another Leaves

Eventually, Jack ran off to Moncton again. He used to call me weekly. He found work driving trucks. One night, the landlord changed the locks on him, and rather than calling and letting me know, he began sleeping rough on park benches. The landlord kept all his possessions and argued the agreement was that the place was to be used for sleeping, not partying with his friends.

I was terrified. Now that Jack was living rough, I lost regular contact with him. Every time the phone rang, I was worried it would be the police calling to tell me they found his body. I decided to go to Moncton and look for him myself. I stayed in a hotel with Debbie, Greg, and another friend named Helen, who helped me find him.

When I knocked on the door, I didn't recognize the person who answered. I was about to ask to speak to Jack when he said, "Mom." He had lost so much weight. He was wearing a toot, and he didn't look like my son at all. He needed a haircut, so I gave him money and arranged a time to go get something to eat. Greg, Helen, Jack, and I ordered steak, and Jack ate like a man possessed. He said he hadn't had a meal like it in months. I know that had I waited even another three months to go find him, I would have lost my son forever. While walking down the street, every time he would see a police officer or car passing, he would tilt his head or try and step into the shadows.

As a show of good faith, I brought him a case of beer to share with his friends one last time. He showed up at the hotel afterward to sleep, and in the morning, I felt it was safe for us to leave.

And so my son returned, and we needed to rent a larger house—a pet-friendly one because while Jack was missing, George had given me a little black kitten that we called John. I called my mother in Greece to let her know that Jack had returned, and she told me that my father was sick of all her medical problems. I asked my father to let her come to Calgary to stay with me. He agreed on the condition that he came over first. On December 9, 1999, we received a call. Mom had passed away. My entire world shifted. I was lost. Liana was with me constantly. All four kids were devastated; they loved her so much. As is the Greek custom, Mom was buried immediately before we had time to travel to see her. Following the burial begins a forty-day period of mourning.

My sister Cat took it particularly bad because our mother died in her house. No one could stop Cat's drama. She kept saying, "I killed her. She died because I was late home to see her." It took Cat a long time to stop blaming herself.

When we arrived in Greece, Guy was waiting to pick us up. He was in tears. He took me straight to Cat's house. Cat collapsed in tears, still blaming herself. I never blamed her. Cat had three small children, including a six-month-old, at the time Mom died, and she could only spread herself so thin. None of us were expecting Mom to pass away; she was unwell, but we thought she would recover.

During the forty-day period of mourning, we all cooked and went to church. We grieved, and we reminisced. Our mother was our tranquilizer. She was our buoy in rough waters.

It was winter during the forty days. It was cold; there was no real heating like there is now, but I made the most of the time I spent back in Greece in getting to know Cat's baby, Tonia, and her other children, Rebecca and Cat. I got to see May's children, Guy and Anna. I had missed them all so much. Andy was in Montreal with her family and still wasn't talking to us.

When the mourning period was over, we headed back to Calgary. Jacky and Senator invited us to their house the night before we left. Liana, Effie, George, Cathy, Helen, Diana, and I spent the evening saying our goodbyes.

Back in Airdrie, we found out my brother-in-law had sold the Ironhorse Restaurant to a cowboy named Dan and his wife, June. They changed the name of the restaurant to the Kicking Horse and appointed a manager and their own chefs. They kept Guy, James, and me on the books. I was up-front and told them they needed to take care of the customers first and foremost. I worked with them for eighteen months. In the beginning, it was wonderful. I introduced them to all the regulars, but their food was no good. They didn't know how to listen, and their Greek salad dressing was made the way Julie liked it, and she was the *only* person who liked it. When I pointed out that customers were complaining about the dressing, my concerns were brushed aside. I often had to take meals back in the kitchen to have Guy fix them up.

In the upstairs bar, they hired strippers and had the servers wear bikinis. June's daughter Loi was one of the dancers. I used to babysit Lor's daughter while she was entertaining customers.

Ltacy was always a clever girl. She worked out that Fridays were when she could make the most money, so she had me watch Thena and John when I was watching Lor's daughter. When the Ironhorse had been sold, we had filed for bankruptcy. It was only Ltacy and I working at the restaurant by that stage. She never gave the children any food, so

I had to cook for them, but I enjoyed having little people in the house again. Jack was doing much better; he was off the hard drugs, although he was still using cannabis.

Jack was a fabulous cook, even better than Guy. So soon, Tom, the manager of the Plaka restaurant, hired him as his right hand. Jack was living with Liana and Ellie, and Liana soon ended up working for Tom too. The Plaka was a great Greek restaurant with a well-deserved name for quality food and service.

During school holidays, my house was the drop-in center for all the kids—even the kids of my friends. I was always cooking salads and appetizers, and after it was all done, they would help me clean up.

Stettler

Every Monday, James and Larry would bring me to Stettler, Alberta, which is a two-hour drive away. There was a Greek man who had a restaurant he ran with his family. I would sit and talk to his family while James and Larry talked to the man. One visit, I overheard them talking about taking over the town pump. I told them I was not leaving Calgary. It was all settled until I had a fight with Liana and asked Larry when we were leaving. There was no getting out of it now. Larry told me I had to give it at least six months. If, after that, I didn't like it, I would return to Airdrie.

Three months after my mother died, shortly after we sold the Ironhorse to the cowboy, my father died in Greece. Don, the cowboy, offered to lend me the money to go to Greece. I declined. When my mother died, he started drinking more heavily and mixing his medication with alcohol and, as a result, suffered a small stroke. I spoke to him in the hospital. Shortly after, he had another more serious stroke that left him paralyzed on the left side of his body. He was already suffering from lung cancer, so the doctors told my sisters Cat and May to take him home and make him comfortable. My daughter, Kat, helped my sisters take care of him; they would run all his food through a blender and feed him with the aid of a straw. In the end, he was catheterized and became completely reliant on others to help him with the toilet and bath. This aspect of his care was particularly hard on May with her past. May once told me that after Uncle Nick took Dad out fishing and questioned him about molesting us, my father held his hand like it was a gun and pointed it at her. I wonder if he thought May had told Uncle Nick. My father never mentioned it to me.

The cancer spread throughout his body and into his brain. Despite the way he had treated me throughout my life and my dislike for him, I did shed a tear, but it was more a tear of relief that finally—finally—he would never hurt me or another child again. I could finally move on with my life. When arrangements in Stettler were finalized, we gave a two-week notice to the Kicking Horse; Don and June only lasted six months without us to look after the customers.

We moved to Stettler in the beginning of July 2002. Our car was so old I have no idea how it made the journey ladened down with all our household goods. Larry had rented the only house available in the town. Stettler was an oil town, so it was filled with oil rig workers. The house had three bedrooms and came with a stove, fridge, washing machine, and dryer. We settled in well. I used to head down and watch the staff at work. We decided to keep Ma, Lat, Betty, V, and Mary's daughter Lara.

Stettler had an old movie theater, a McDonald's, a Dairy Queen, a Walmart, and us. With just over five thousand people in the town, the vast majority of them being farmers, there was a lot of emphasis on trying to keep the money in Stettler. There was no reason Stettler couldn't be a completely self-sufficient town; they have dairy cows, sheep, goats, llamas, buffalo, and beef farms as well as native moose and ducks, which were available during hunting seasons.

For the first few months of operating, we didn't draw salary from the restaurant, so we could get an indication of where we stood financially. In August of 2002, George, my father-in-law, passed away. It was a terrible loss. We were all so upset. We were unable to leave the restaurant to attend his mourning, so we did our own private mourning at home.

In Crete, Aunt Mary had an accident and was set afire. The neighbors heard and came running to help. Uncle Tony took her to the hospital. The burns were severe enough that she needed to be transported to Athens. The shock and pain caused her the almost instant onset of dementia. Tony's side of the family convinced her to sign her half of the house deed over to them. Tony sold the property, and to his credit, he did share the profits with my aunt's family. With the money I received, I was able to purchase a lovely two-story three-bedroom house. The house had three bathrooms, a large living area, a fully equipped kitchen, a large backyard, and a cute little front. It was our home for a decade before I sold it and downsized.

James convinced Jack to leave the Plaka and come work for us. It was like putting a cat in with a tiger. Jack made a friend named Tan; to begin with, it was okay. She had a house of her own, and he would stay with her on occasion. Then once again, he gravitated toward a bad crowd and started to use cocaine again. He was missing shifts at work, although James was still paying him against my wishes. I turned up at Tan's house with clean clothes to try and get Jack to come to work, but it was near impossible to wake him. Tan had him sleeping in the basement with no mattress. He was unkempt; his clothes were unwashed. My heart was breaking. Every day I was terrified I was going to lose him forever. So many people had overdosed and died in Tan's house; I didn't want my son to be next. Every day, I would practically hold my breath until the afternoon, waiting to see if Jack would arrive at work. I used to try and help by finding his drug suppliers and threatening them to leave him alone and bailing up his so-called friends who would do drugs with him to try and talk sense into them. Tan was addicted to prescription painkillers. Jack and Tan were always trying to scam money out of James and me by claiming they needed repairs for their car or that the bathroom had flooded and they needed a plumber, but it always went on drugs.

James' Fight

I n 2004, James went to the doctor for a checkup and was diagnosed with colon cancer. It was very unexpected. James looked as fit as an ox. He never smoked, didn't drink, and was a healthy eater. He was booked to have a colonoscopy. I rushed out and bought all the books on cancer I could find locally to try to understand what was happening and what to expect.

After the colonoscopy, when we came home, James began to hemorrhage. There was blood everywhere. I rushed him back to the hospital where he was admitted to surgery and stayed in the hospital for another week. When James awoke from surgery, he was in agony. In all the years I've known him, he never so much as took an aspirin. He had such a high tolerance for pain, so for him to be demanding painkillers, it must have been excruciating. One of the books I had read mentioned clots. They hadn't given James anything to stop blood clots. Finally, they gave him compression stockings, and it helped somewhat with the circulation, but it was a little too late. He already had blood clots, and his stomach was swollen. They have to move him to the larger Alexandra Hospital in Edmonton, which was two hours away.

Saving James' life was hard. He was intubated, and he fought hard against it. He had to be sedated before they could successfully insert the tube. His legs were full of clots and, as a result, suffered from ulcerations. I was with James constantly. I was exhausted. One night, Guy came to pick me up. James chucked a tantrum and yelled that I couldn't leave; I was his maid. That was devastating to me. I walked out and went home with George. I headed to the bathroom to try and soak away my sadness. The next day, I pulled myself back together and went back to the hospital. While we were in the hospital, Mike called from Greece to discuss opening another restaurant with us. When James came home three days later, we had to move Jack into the basement as he had broken out in shingles. James and I decided to let Larry open a restaurant with Mike, taking him up on the offer to open a restaurant in Greece. So in the summer, Larry headed to Greece to help Mike get ready.

Two years after the colonoscopy, James started to bleed from the mouth. He'd gone out shopping with Joseph, the man we bought the town pump from. They were in Red Deer, a town an hour away from Stettler. I'm certain the grocery shopping trip was just a cover so they could go to the casino. When they got home, he was still bleeding, so I took him to the local hospital. The doctor on duty tried to tell me it was just a nosebleed. I left James in the hospital for the night and asked the nurses to call me if the bleeding continued.

At the restaurant the next day, Liana and I prepared the homemade soups for the day, and once they were simmering away, I headed to the hospital to pick up James since no one had called me. When I got there, I found he was still bleeding. I raised some level of hell, and the doctors came running and decided to call for the medical helicopter to transport James to Calgary. I followed in my car. It was a two-hour drive. By the time I arrived, my niece Lacy came running out to tell me James' condition was listed as critical and that he wasn't expected to survive. His doctor came out and advised me to notify his family. I alerted a few in Canada and let them notify those in the United States and Greece.

They worked on James for over twelve hours. Our kids arrived as soon as they could. Two days later, his sister Cat and my sister Cat came to stay for a week. It took eight or nine days until the blood loss finally stopped; unfortunately, it only stopped because James developed a clot in his lung. Once the clot was removed, the uncontrolled bleeding began again. I didn't want to leave him for a minute, but everyone was pushing me to go home and shower, and at that point, I was still too quiet to push back and make waves.

Larry flew in from Greece and came directly to the hospital before heading up to check on the restaurant. I told my son and his brothers that if he did die, I would bury James in Greece in the village he loved.

Dr. Mithou was James' doctor. She was from Montreal and was also a professor at Foothills Hospital. She refused to give up. She put James in an induced coma and had a Catholic priest come and do a blessing. The doctors put in a filter near his hip to clear away the clots before they hit main organs, but he was still unconscious. One evening, Dr. Mithou came to see me and told me that he wouldn't survive the night. I spoke to him and told him that we needed him. We needed him to fight. By some miracle, he survived the night and awoke the next morning. We were ecstatic. When he saw the two Cathys over from Greece, he asked them what they were doing in Canada. Within a few days, he was back to his old self again. They took him out of the intensive care unit and removed the feeding tubes. When we left the hospital, the two Cats headed back to Greece.

It's Not Your Fault, Mom

J ack had invited his friend Jim from Moncton. Jim was working as a dish hand in the restaurant. Jim had gotten heavily involved in heroin and was trying to get himself clean. Jack was staying with Tan, so Jim stayed with us in Jack's bedroom. Unfortunately, Jim stole Jack's jewelry and used it to buy drugs. Both Jack and Jim were on hard drugs again, although since Jack had an aversion to needles, he never injected drugs. I couldn't handle dealing with Jim and his drug use and thieving ways, so I contacted his mother and asked her what I should do with him. She asked me to bring him to Edmonton where there was a detox and drug rehabilitation center.

I found out it was one of our older waitresses who had been giving Jim painkillers and started his addiction. I don't know if she pushed drugs on Jack or not; I didn't give her the chance to explain. I pushed her out the door. I sat Jack down and demanded the truth. He told me he had tried all the drugs I was aware of and a few I'd never even heard of. When I took Jim to Edmonton, Jack decided to leave Tan. He was fed up with living in the basement in filthy conditions and with minimal food available. He came home. He was addicted to crack cocaine.

When Jack was using, he was as white as a ghost. He walked around like a zombie—moving but not really animated. He saw my face one day and said to me, "It's not your fault, Mom. It's not your fault I am a junkie." That killed me. I was the one who had been giving him money. He was using that money to purchase drugs. I was playing a role in the death of my son. One morning, he came into my room and asked me for money. I gave it to him, so he didn't end up stealing something. Once he left, I felt so guilty that I took paroxetine. I wanted to kill myself. I no longer cared. I had no support from anyone.

I realized I needed help, so I spoke to a police officer about Jack. He said he was aware of Jack and his thieving, but they had been unable to prove it. They had not caught him red-handed.

In 2005, James and I headed to Greece. They took us to Marathi—the new restaurant that Mike and Larry had set up. They had prepared a meal fit for kings, and both sides of the family were there. I met my sister Cat's kids for the first time: Cat, Rebe, and Anto. Once we had eaten, I went swimming at the beach with Thena, my sister-in-law Cat, and little Anto.

It was a wonderful time, seeing everyone whom I had missed over the past few years and spoiling my nieces. I bought Anto a Miley Cyrus / Hannah Montana backpack and a beach towel. She was excited to be the first kid in Chania to have it. Anto dared me to walk home from the shops barefoot and was shocked and giggled when I did and couldn't wait to race in and tell her mother about crazy Auntie Debbie.

I loved all my nieces and nephews beyond words. Mary's children were now grown. Ioan is a lovely-looking girl, and my nephew Guy, just twenty-four days older than my Guy, was a true Greek; he was such a wild boy with a heart of gold. I also enjoyed spending time with James's family; we were constantly at the beach with my sister-in-law Cat and Thena or at Mike's restaurant, which overlooked the beach. We would often stay there until evening. Polly's children—Natasha, George, James, and Steve—were all similar ages to my own children.

Her children never gave her a moment's bother. She did a phenomenal job in raising her children. I loved being around Polly and her beautiful children.

Eventually, it was time to go home. I never got my head around the Crete mentality. I knew going home would mean I had a lot of paperwork to catch up on and that I was going to have to give my staff time off to cover all the additional shifts they had to work while we were away and dealing with James's illness.

Cuba, Constantinople, and Seeing the World

S tettler was nice after Christmas. In February, I left for Cuba with Soula and my niece Ltacy. I enjoyed the beach, but my favorite pastime was watching people interact with one another. Each day, I would ride the bus and watch the people in all the different areas of Cuba, including the impoverished people living in dilapidated concrete buildings. Cuba was still communist. Castro was still in power.

At ten o'clock each evening, they had a different show. Some were so funny you would think you were going to die laughing. I stayed in Cuba for a week. It was a different life. The resort was very beautiful; it had a mini rainforest with many exotic birds, coconuts, bananas, papayas, and mangoes. The evening buffet was a mixture of Canadian and Cuban foods.

Cat really took a liking to piña coladas, and when I say she overindulged, she *really* overindulged. She had no idea how drunk she was. She would try to tease and humiliate men in front of my daughter, Kat. Kat ended up just as embarrassed as the men were.

At 10:00 p.m. each night, security would shut the beaches. I had been given clear instructions by the menfolk back home to stock up on Cuban cigars, so I bought a few and some good rum. When we were on the plane heading home, Cat was sitting next to a lady who continually sprayed herself with Lysol. We thought it was odd, but it didn't really bother us too much until she started spraying on Cat. Cat developed a complex and asked whether her feet smelled. It turned out the woman had smelly gas and was trying to disguise the smell. The people sitting behind Cat kept kicking her chair thinking she was responsible for the stench. The air stewardess eventually gave the woman something to settle her stomach.

Once back in Stettler, I had to work double shifts to allow staff time off. I was running between both the restaurant and the lounge until my daughter Kat turned up for her shift at 5:00 p.m. If the lounge got busy throughout the night, I had to run back up there.

In August, Thena, Cat, and I traveled to Constantinople, Turkey. It was a remarkable city. There were millions of people, stunning architectures, and so many beautiful and expensive clothing boutiques. Again, my love of people watching had me board a tour bus where I saw less fortunate people who slept on the streets. The food was similar to that of Greek cuisine; the sweet pastry dishes were delicious. The fish was also very good. The coffee was the best, though. I am very particular with my coffee, and I was more than pleased with it. I couldn't say the same for their driving, though. I think they might have been the worst drivers I've ever seen in my life.

Constantinople had an enormous open-air market filled with exotic spices I'd never even heard of, and caviar was freely available to taste. They sold hookahs, knickknacks, and beautiful glassware. The travel bug had hit. I was only back in Canada until February before I was to head back to Cuba, this time with Athena.

Jerusalem, Lebanon, and Egypt

My house had become a hellhole. My husband, brother-in-law, and a friend and his wife would get together every evening to play cards. I was working from six in the morning until eight in the evening, dealing with the public and heaving loads of plates from the restaurant and the lounge. They didn't seem to care. Lyn was a great blessing. Her advice was sage. She told me to lock myself in my room, have a bubble bath, and try to forget they were there. This carried on seven days a week for five years. I asked James countless times to stop it, but as usual, it was in one ear and out the other.

Monday was my only day off. I would clean the house and do the laundry as quickly as I could and then run upstairs and hide in my room until one to two in the morning.

After the first year of card games, I headed to Jerusalem in the summer. It was great. I was with my sisters-in-law. They were my travel companions again. When we landed, the heat almost took my breath away. The Holy Land was filled with tourists and was surprisingly peaceful. The Israelis were kind. Our hotel was one of the nicer ones I'd stayed in, and the shopping district was filled with good-quality clothing stores. The food was great—lots of yogurts, pita breads, olives, lamb and goat meat, and wonderful aromatic coffee and teas. The open markets were among the best I've seen.

My sisters and I were traveling with four other couples. Getting to know them was enjoyable. I went to the Jordan River and just lay silently in the river while looking at all the people who were with me. There were so many people from diverse walks of life all waiting to be baptized; it was amazing. I enjoyed it a lot and have no regrets about going there. We traveled to Lebanon for a day trip together. Lebanon was very similar to Israel except that it was a little more progressive with women's attire, although women still wore the religious coverings. We felt the women were allowed a little more freedom in Lebanon; there were even nightclubs.

When walking the backstreets, you could see older women all in black sitting on the ground, cooking pita bread the traditional way using a large grinding rock, then cooking it in a man-made outdoor wood-fired oven. My sisters and companions went to the disco and casino, and I went to the hotel to catch up on sleep.

We also traveled to Egypt where we went to a perfume store where they made and exported perfume to the rest of the world and to a papyrus store where they showed us the traditional way to make papyrus. I had no idea that so much work went into creating a single sheet of paper. I purchased quite a few sheets of paper and bottles of perfume (which I never actually used. I just got caught up in the buying hype). I toured the pyramids and museums. I was fascinated by the mummies and the golden statues of the cats.

There were so many mosques, but I only ever saw men entering. They would wash their hands, feet, and faces and enter without shoes on their feet. We visited Mount Sinai where Moses received the Ten Commandments.

At the end of our tour of the Middle East, I decided the Jewish people were warm and kind as were the Lebanese people. Egypt was dirty, and I was afraid to walk on my own. The men were lecherous.

When the tour finished, we headed back to Greece. My brain kept going over all I'd seen—how the women were only allowed to speak in public with other women, how the men only interacted with men, and how you could only speak to your husband in the privacy of your own home, certainly not openly in the streets. I didn't stay long in Greece. I needed to head back home to Canada.

Ireland

I was still seeing Lyn at this stage, and Jack was still with Diane and was doing very well. He'd even managed to put on a little much-needed weight. He was always on the thin side compared to Guy and Kat who were more solidly built.

James was still gambling. He would try and blame Larry for his inability to stop, and likewise, Larry would blame James. I had to learn to accept it. They were Greek and will always be Greek. I suffered from paroxysmal depolarizing shift—a preseizure neuronal spike in epilepsy for which I am on medication. Lyn advised me to see a psychologist. He told me that James was the problem and that as long as I am with him, I will never get better. Ha. It's easy for him to say. I had no way of surviving without James's income. So I continued to work. I developed close relationships with my customers. We joked and laughed, and my days would go by like this. Come nightfall, I would hope not to see any of them. I hated the screams, the cards, the triumphs, and the tantrums. The card games made my heart race, and I don't know why.

I worked all winter through summer, and then in October, I tried desperately to convince my sister Cat and her teenage daughter Anto to go with me to Ireland. Cat is so stubborn; she didn't want to come because she didn't have the money to spare and kept saying no. I gave her no option and booked and paid for her ticket from Athens to Ireland.

I arrived one day ahead of Cat and Anto, so I went out for breakfast and went outside to wait for them to arrive. I knew I was going to love Ireland. It was so green. There was a river directly opposite the hotel. The people were so friendly; they would say hello as they walked by.

Cat and Anto also fell in love with Ireland and said it was like a dream. Anto was ravenous when she got off the plane and wanted to eat McDonald's or Burger King. We went to eat and then spent the day walking around Ireland. We went to the Guinness Storehouse. I fell down some stairs; it frightened my family, but I wasn't too badly injured.

Everywhere we went, we fell in love. We found a statue of a girl named Molly. During the day, Molly was a fishmonger girl. During the evening hours, she was a lady of the night. We all bought one. That evening, we went to the pub for dinner.

The breakfast buffet the next morning was phenomenal. Anto loved it. Cat was a little disturbed by the blood pudding. And for me, there was nothing better than the coffee. It was like velvet. After breakfast, we went for a walk and saw a lake with swans peacefully gliding around. I can't describe how majestic it was. We took Anto to the zoo and were startled by three old men. We jumped, and they laughed. Soon we were all laughing so hard we almost peed ourselves. Later, we found ourselves in a position to return the favor and startled the three gents. Thankfully, they saw the humor in it, and no one had a heart attack!

That evening, we went to a pub that had live music for a little while, but we had to head to the motel because we had an early morning. Cat and Anto were looking forward to the morning buffet again. It was October 29, and all of Ireland was making preparations for Samhain— the Celtic pagan version of Halloween. Having grown up in Greece, Antonia had little knowledge of Halloween, so it was exciting for her. We enjoyed treating her to different Halloween treats, like the cupcakes decorated like jack-o'-lanterns. We went on a Samhain tour bus and visited historical graveyards. I never thought I'd see the day I would think it was fun to take photos of old tombstones, but there I was doing just that. They took us to the site where the famous box office hit movie *P.S. I Love You* was filmed. It was even more breathtaking in person than it was in the film. Dublin was amazing. Surrounded by mountains and the ocean, it was ethereal. The food was nice; they use a lot of butter and fish. I ordered fish and chips and was given more than enough to feed two people.

We took a tour to Belfast, which was such a contrast to Dublin. You could sense the presence of drugs and guns everywhere. It was dirty. There were huge malls, and everything was overpriced. No one talked to anyone; they just looked at the ground or out the side of their eyes. Gangs of punks walked around and tagged the name of their gang on walls. The tour included a visit to the IRA stomping grounds. We went to historical jails and talked a little about the history of the IRA and how many people on either side of this war were harmed or killed. It was truly horrific to learn how religion was behind all this suffering.

When it was time to leave Ireland, I was supposed to head directly to Canada, but my daughter was involved with a guy in Greece whom I knew was crazy, and I knew his ex-girlfriend who had told me the same. One night, I saw him while we were out. I told everyone he was crazy and told my daughter that if she marries him, her life will be the same as the one I had—filled with beatings, gambling, drugs, and sadness. There was no doubt about it; he'd already beaten his first wife. Thank God she listened to me and didn't marry him. If she had, I'd have ridden roughshod all over him, though.

Working with Lyn on a monthly basis meant that I was gradually becoming more sensible and learning coping strategies to deal with stress. Originally, when something was upsetting me, I would retreat to my bedroom, watch the TV loudly, then take a sleeping pill. I no longer do these things. I have healthier coping mechanisms.

It wasn't always rosy at the restaurant either. At work, we would argue with the kids. George would get angry with me for not being a runner when I was spreading myself thin in the dining room and the lounge. I had to help Kat; she was alone and needed her tables cleaned. Guy was very much my son. When he gets mad, he retreats into himself and will be silent. He can hold his grudge for days. Kat is similar. Jack is the only one who pushes you to communicate and make sure that everything is okay. The only time we felt like an actual family were the religious holidays, such as Christmas and Easter. During those periods, we thoroughly enjoyed one another's company.

In November 2011, I bought my sister a ticket to Calgary; and then my sister, daughter, and I headed to Cuba. Cuba had changed remarkably since the last time I was there when there were a lot of drugs and young women being visibly sold on the streets. It was a surprise to see it had now become a social country. Castro was still alive, but he was unwell. His brother was now running the country. It was my sister's first time in Cuba, and she loved the resort. We had a lovely two-bedroom apartment, and housekeeping came daily to straighten up the room for us. We enjoyed multiple daily piña coladas and ate three decent meals a day. However, the constant exposure to the sun dehydrated the body a lot, so we had to make a conscious effort to remember to drink lots of water.

We had many laughs. It was wonderful to spend time together. One night, it was raining. And I can't recall exactly how it came to happen, but Cat was locked outside by herself, and she started to laugh. We laughed so hard that we actually peed ourselves. We had to hurriedly clean the floor outside the door before the guests in the room next to ours noticed and complained. We cleaned it up and then called the reception to say we'd dropped a jug of water and the floor was now wet. The next day, we rented a Jeep to get away from the resort for the day. We went sightseeing. Cat was pleased that she got to drive the Jeep. She felt free. She loved driving, especially at night. She was also quite friendly and invited people to sit with us, including married men who were looking for a good time. Quite a few times, I delivered a swift kick to her ankle under the table to remind her to behave herself. She tried hard to behave herself, but it was a struggle.

Around the World

The travel bug bit me hard. There is something magical about visiting other countries, peeking into their world, and experiencing the things they take for granted. Of all the places I had been, one of my favorites was Constantinople. It was clean with lots of green areas and date trees. Fresh dates were available everywhere. Once you've eaten a fresh date, you'll never want to eat a dry one again. The people drove erratically though, and terrifyingly so. I don't think I've witnessed driving like it in any other country. The buildings were spectacular, especially the Hagia Sophia Cathedral. It is painted gold on the exterior and contains a lot of gold relics inside. It is an ancient Greek Orthodox church that is being transformed into a mosque, which you need to pay to enter. It takes over three hours to complete the tour; it is so large. Turkey has so much history.

Tea and coffee leaf readers walk the streets offering to read your fortune, and you can see the Bosphorus Bridge, which divides Russia and Turkey. At night, it lights up and is filled with nightclubs and belly dancers.

Las Vegas is a city that never sleeps. My sister-in-law Athena and her daughter Lacy love to gamble, and they convinced me to go to Nevada with them. We'd get up early for breakfast, and then I'd sit around waiting until they'd finished gambling before we headed off to see the sights. Las Vegas was really expensive and very busy, but it was nice. The hotel we stayed in had a nice waterfront with colored lights that changed with the music. Tourists from all over the globe flocked to the casinos. We saw a Cirque du Soleil show; it was unbelievable. I enjoyed it tremendously. Following that show was a live show with knights on horseback. Our food was brought to us, and we ate with our hands while we enjoyed the show. We also visited Madame Tussauds wax museum and saw Elvis, Rocky, and Diana, Princess of Wales. Each one was so lifelike. There was also a hotel shaped just like the pyramids of Cairo.

Detox

I n the winter, Jack decided to detoxify. I found him curled up like a
ball in pain. I asked if he needed anything. He said no. I still went
out and bought him a pile of sweets and Pepsi. I read somewhere that
they can crave sweet foods during detox. I sat beside him as he ate the
sweets and watched him suffer. It was something I wish no other mother
ever has to experience. I approached a mental health organization to
come and help me in the house with Jack. They sent a short man with
salt-and-pepper gray hair and beard to the house to talk to me. I gave
him a brief rundown, and he fobbed me off and indicated that John
was in the position he is in because of his own choices.

Here I was, desperate for help, and I was being refused because my
son was a twenty-eight-year-old adult. My child is my child regardless
of his age. He offered me an appointment. I accepted it though I knew
full well I would not be attending. I did, however, turn up and stood
outside the building for what felt like ages before one of the workers,
Lyn, saw me and escorted me inside. Lyn was compassionate. She
made me feel comfortable and relaxed. Before long, I felt comfortable
enough to discuss Jack with her. Lyn said something similar to what
the man with salt-and-pepper hair said—that Jack's position is solely
of Jack's doing and is not my fault. But she followed it up by asking
whether I wanted her to help me get better. I met with Lyn twice a

week in the beginning. She had a gentle way of asking questions, and I felt safe enough to answer. Mostly, I talked about my father. It was like a monster leaving my soul. The trauma meant that I was having bed-wetting accidents at night, which was really embarrassing as I was sharing a bed with James. In all, I saw Lyn for seven years.

In January 2007, we were kicked out of the restaurant due to the fact that we had very good revenue and they kicked us out and brought new owners in the restaurant. There were six people without a job, and it was impossible to make him see reason. There was another restaurant nearby whose owner we knew, and he let us rent it. But it needed a lot of work from top to bottom. We left the design with the men, and I headed off to the Dominican Republic with my daughter, some of my sisters-in-law, and my nieces. It was not as nice as Cuba; the nightlife was not as vibrant, and the coffee was terrible. The grapefruit was interesting, though; it was sweet instead of bitter. I liked it a lot. We were only in the Dominican Republic for a week. My impression is that the people were lazy. They had so many workable fruits and vegetables to make money, but they didn't utilize them. The resorts brought in the money.

When we returned to Stettler, we helped the men with the final touches on the new restaurant. We opened the doors for the first evening on March 20. It was packed. All our original customers had come back to us.

In the summer the next year, I headed back to Greece to see my sisters, and together, we traveled to Barcelona in Spain. We arrived late, and I was so tired. I fell asleep right away, but I did notice the room was pretty bad. My sisters decided to go complain at the office while I was sleeping and were given upgrades to two much nicer rooms with kitchenettes. Barcelona's history dates back to the 1500s, and the churches and museums were stunning. Cat was fascinated and insisted we visit all the art galleries, churches, and museums we could.

One afternoon, we were sitting outside the colosseum when this very handsome man with emerald-green eyes, olive skin, and long dark hair walked past. We all stared at him. Cat sashayed right up to him and told him how handsome we all thought he was; she had no shame! He thanked her graciously and left.

Cat was still beautiful. We all nearly died laughing one morning when we were sitting on a bench outside in the sun when a much older man came and sat beside Cat and tried to make a very blatant pass at her. He even tried to show her he had a wallet full of money to persuade her.

In all, Barcelona was very nice. There was sexual freedom, gay bars, and sex workers. The nightlife was open well into the wee hours of the morning. We went to the stadium to watch soccer and bought the boys jerseys. We did a lot of walking; our legs were so tired at the end of each day. The cuisine was different—interesting. I particularly loved tapas.

I was tired of shopping for clothes and sightseeing, so while my sisters headed off to do that, I found an open market full of meat, fish, vegetables, flowers, and fabrics.

My sisters loved to torment me about my weak bladder, and one night at a restaurant, I could not hold it in. My sisters and nieces literally fell on the floor in hysterics. I take diuretic pills and found myself needing desperately to urinate. I tried to ask a few people where the nearest public restroom was, but no one could understand me. Desperate, I hid behind two very large garbage dumpsters, lifted my skirt, and peed. We fled the restaurant, taking my tapas with me. I was really annoyed at them to begin with, but looking back, even I laugh about it now.

The weather in Spain was stunning—beautiful and warm. In contrast, the Spaniards were kind of cold and do not speak English. Once, we went to watch a flamenco dance, and although it was executed to perfection, the performers never smiled. I always bought gifts back for my staff and for Lyn. I preferred to buy the gifts from the country we visited, whereas my sisters liked to shop in the duty-free section at the airport.

Back in Canada, Jack met a girl named Dia at a staff party. She was married at the time but was undergoing a divorce. I credit her with saving my son. She got him off the hard drugs, and he was only smoking weed. They were together for ten years. I think Jack was crazy for breaking up with her. She was lovely, and I cared for her like a daughter.

Independence

B ack in Stettler, nothing had changed. I decided to leave for Montreal for good. Debbie could take care of herself. My entire marriage had never been more than a giant high-pitched squealing match. I was over it. My insides felt constantly knotted. I was fed up with the continual card games, the forgotten meals on the cooktop that would set off the smoke detectors, and the god-awful screaming and hooting. You'd think they were playing for high stakes.

On February 28, 2016, I packed my suitcase and walked out the door. I headed to my sister Andy's house. Andy and Notie had a spare room, and they graciously let me stay with them. It was a pleasing room with a large window that received the sun almost all day long.

When I woke up in the mornings, Andy would already have fresh coffee brewing. We'd chat over a cup and would then clean up before heading to the kitchen to prepare the day's meals. Andy had a little dog, Cookie. I loved her, but unfortunately, in Montreal, if you're a smoker or have a dog, it is near impossible to find a rental house. So I just enjoy playing with Cookie at Andy's house. One day, when the weather was nice, I insisted Andy bring Cookie along on a walk with us. We walked for over an hour. Poor Cookie was so pooped we had to carry her home, and she went right to sleep and didn't move all night.

When Andy would go to work, I'd set about doing all the housework so that when she came home, she could sit and relax. At times, I would go stay with Aunt Virginia to help her care for my cousin Cathy, who was now in her fifties but who was mentally eight years old. Cathy's brother Tasso was now a pilot for the Royal Canadian Mounted Police. He, his wife, and his son Manolios would come and visit. The nights were worst with Cathy. Nightfall would unsettle her, and she would become violent. She used to regularly attack my uncle.

Each Saturday, I would stay with my cousin Liana, and I would leave each Sunday to go back to Andy's. Liana loved to cook for me all the things I loved to eat—bread and buttery and fatty food. I started to gain weight, so as soon as the weather improved in March, Andy and I started walking for an hour each day. By April, we were walking two to three hours each day. I had a fast walking pace, and Andy struggled to keep up at times.

I would call my kids often and cry about how much I missed them. I never wanted to be the crazy mother, but here I was! Guy had sold the restaurant, so I was a free bird; there was nothing holding me back. My medication was costing me $500 per month, so I decided to go home to Greece and get my house ready. The house was beautiful; it had all the modern conveniences. My daughter and sister Cat decided to travel to Italy to see Florence and invited me and my sister-in-law Cat along. I thought, *Why not?* The night before we were due to leave, I fell over and cracked a rib. I couldn't walk without pain. We only went for a few days, but they were the worst few days of my life! All my sister-in-law wanted to do was shop. She wasn't interested in seeing any of the sights in Florence. We left her to her shopping, and we went and saw the Italian monuments and the beautiful statues of the gods and goddesses of Roman mythology. We ate fresh prosciutto sandwiches, and we went to the Leaning Tower of Pisa. I did all this while in excruciating agony because of my broken rib.

When we returned to Crete, Kat was still staying with me, and Guy came to visit. They both loved the house in Crete; it was the first time they saw it. I had bought a parcel of land near my sister Cat's house. Oh boy, did James lose his cool when I chose to build on it rather than on his land, but I wanted something for myself—something he couldn't take and destroy or lose in one of his stupid gambling matches. My home in Crete was five minutes from the seaside and close to restaurants if you didn't feel like cooking. It is peaceful. I enjoy relaxing there and drinking coffee and reading novels. I have no one to talk to, but reading is a relaxing pastime that I enjoy. My love for books didn't rub off on my children, although I tried to promote books and reading to them throughout their childhood; the boys have so many books that I gifted them just sitting unopened in their rooms. Perhaps they'll read this one, though. I can't say for sure about Kathy. Kathy's always been a very private person. She has always liked her own company and has lived independently since she was seventeen when she left to go to college.

In all my travels, my favorite thing to do was observe people. I always look directly into someone's eyes. I know it makes some people uncomfortable, but it is the easiest way for me to judge the quality of a person.

The waiters in Greece were the least intrusive but also the least friendly of all the waitstaff I have interacted with in my travels. They would deliver the food and beverages and leave; they never asked how you enjoyed your meal or came to clean away the dishes and glassware. They would leave it all on the table until you have left the venue. Being a waitress, I can't help myself. I have to stack everything neatly in the corner of the table to make it neat.

I am currently seeing the counselor again due to atrial fibrillation (AFib). During my last attack, I was sent to the hospital, and they worked on ways to reduce my heart rate. They wanted me to stay in for a few days, but I refused and went home. The next day, I fell to the floor sobbing and realized I needed help. I needed someone to talk to, so I started seeing a counselor.

Opening Up

I n 2014, I felt brave enough to begin to tell some of my in-laws my secret. I had felt dirty for so many years for holding this secret inside. I kept asking everyone for forgiveness. Everyone said, "It's not your fault," but as the child who had been abused, it never leaves you. Watching the evening news or reading the daily newspaper can be a trigger if there is a story about another child being abused. My blood boils, and I want to kill the person responsible.

Years earlier, in Stettler, I entrusted my secret with one of my waitresses. I didn't consider Pat as just one of my waitresses; I considered her a close friend. So when I found out that she had told others what I had shared with her in confidence, I was very hurt. The betrayal shattered my trust in people.

Back in Crete, I worked long hours in the restaurant and carried a lot of weight—empty plates can really weigh up when you're carrying nine or ten plates at a time. When my staff were sick, I covered their shifts. I rarely took time off for myself. I loved my customers.

John was using drugs again, thanks to Jack. Jake had stolen most of John's gold when he was staying at our house and sold it to buy drugs. In 2013, one of John's friends, Mike, called to speak to John. John wasn't home, and I promised to get John to return the call. I truly forgot to pass the message on. The next day, Cat called John and said that Mike had committed suicide. I still carry the guilt for this.

Sometimes, I like to reminisce about the past years; some of my favorite memories involve the antics the little ones got up to. When Electra was small, she had a stash of chocolates. My mother asked if she would share some with her grandmother. Electra ran from the room yelling, "No, I'm not giving you any!" Oh, I still laugh at the memory. My nephew Mike would hide my mother's walking stick and pretend he knew nothing about it. His little face would turn red, and his ears would wiggle from trying so hard not to laugh. Another favorite memory was the time Andy dyed Mom's hair, but it turned out carrot red. Mom was horrified to begin with but grew to like it over time.

Sometimes I would remember memories that are not so pleasant, like how controlling my father was. He controlled my mother, and he controlled us three girls. It scares me to wonder how he would have treated us if we didn't have the other males in our lives looking out for us. We protected Cathy ourselves. We never left her alone with our father. Every weekend, she would stay at either my house or May's. Cathy and Ann were afforded privileges that Mary and I were not, like riding bicycles and swimming in neighbors' pools. I remember the time Ann painted her fingernails and my father took out a knife and made her scrape it off. I was so tense throughout the whole episode—terrified he was going to beat me for allowing her to do it. One night, we were eating bean soup. Mary hated bean soup and was complaining about it. He took her head, pushed her face into the bowl, and belted her backside with his strap. He then made her sit down and finish eating the soup.

When I went to Greece in 2016, my sister was working at her hotel. I don't remember why we went into the city, but we did, and we headed to her house for a siesta. We started chatting, and Cathy was complaining about how she could never understand why Mary, Ann, and I hated our father. I never set out to tell her, but before I knew it, I was telling her everything. She was devastated. Her entire perception of him was shattered. She vomited. She begged us not to tell her daughters—not to destroy the memory of their grandfather. Cathy called Mary, and Mary confirmed my stories. Cathy was so angry with us. Mary explained that all we wanted to do was protect her. We didn't want her to be like us who, whenever we got together, inevitably ended up discussing him.

Mary and Ann's husbands still did not know about the sexual abuse. Mary had suffered enough with Nick beating her and cheating on her, but for the past fifteen years, he's been a good husband. He cooks, he takes care of Mary, and he takes her wherever he goes. Nick came from a good family; his father was a shepherd, and he adored Nick's mother.

Ann was brainwashed. Her husband's brother had tried to rape her. She called my house in hysterics, and James raced to her house and kicked out Ann's brother-in-law. He was using drugs, but he never went to Ann's house again. Ann had very little to do with us. Notie tried to control the amount of contact she had with us. I am glad things are different now, and we are able to communicate more freely. Mary's one fault is that she's always borrowing money. There is a recession in Greece right now, so there isn't a lot of money, so we all have to help Mary out at times.

Debbie's Dreams

My dream is to have a different life for my sister and for me to receive a doll at Christmas. I may be sixty-two years old, but this wish has stayed with me all my years. I wish I never had to see my mother get beaten. I wish she didn't have to work the long hours that she did. I wish that she had been spoken to with kindness. My dream was to have a father like the father in the storybooks we read at school—ones who cared about and protected their families. My dream was to finish the twelfth grade. My most desired wish is that I have not abused my own children—that I did not bring my children up in the environment they were raised in. My dream is to stop fearing that my youngest will lose his ongoing battle with substance abuse. I dream of a husband who knows what color my eyes are without having to check, one who notices when I have had a haircut.

In the forty-four years James and I have been married, I have never heard a nice word from his mouth. This might seem like a trivial complaint, but it makes my heart ache. That's not to say my life hasn't seen its share of success. When we sold the restaurant in Stettler, we made local history; they covered the sale in the paper. I was so happy; people cared about me and were proud of me. Forty-six years ago, when I first met James, he was a gentleman. He cared about me, and he wasn't afraid to show it. As time passed, though, he became this colder version of my husband who was only animated when playing cards. He shared none of the household responsibilities and left the rearing of the children to me. He barely helped at the restaurant.

Each summer, my nieces Cathy, Rebecca, and Antonia—my sister Cathy's children—would help out in the hotel. I'm pretty sure they thought their Auntie Debbie was crazy.

My elementary schooling years were good. The only thing I feared back then was being hit with the belt. I enjoyed school; it taught me manners. And although I could recognize that ours was not a functional family, I learned what a family should be. At lunch, we'd head home and do our homework while we watched *The Flintstones* and then we'd head back to school for the afternoon session. I was a good student. I always received good grades. I particularly loved learning languages. French was my favorite.

In 1986, when I was having some issues with my thyroid, they injected my body with iodine. During the blood test analysis, they realized I was pregnant. The gynecologist recommended I have an abortion because the iodine could cause major birth defects to the baby. They gave me a date to have the termination. My sister Cathy and sister-in-law Cathy came with me. When the procedure was over, I asked the doctor if it was a boy or a girl, but my sister-in-law said it was best I didn't know. This was during the decade when we were living in Greece and James was spending all his time playing cards and encouraging me to join. I felt it was such a waste of time and was terrified that I might play the wrong card and that he would verbally berate me in front of everyone. I was constantly tense.

Xia, my sister-in-law, was married to a naval ship mechanic who was away for months at a time. Each month, she would travel six hours by boat to the navy department to collect his wages. She was such a levelheaded, sensible girl. I loved to spend time with her and her daughter Cathy. As Xia was pregnant with her second child, I went to spend three weeks with her to take care of Cathy while she rested. When she went into labor, I took her to the hospital and was with her when she gave birth to a little boy named Nick. The staff at the hospital joked that I was the father.

Xia's husband, John, came that night. The navy flew him home. He was so, so happy to have a son. Xia raised her children to have beautiful manners. Every summer, we would get together and head to the beach with all our children. One day, I opened up and told Xia about my abuse. Xia was so upset and found it hard to contain her tears. Cathy, my daughter, was also very emotional about it. The boys compartmentalized their feelings and showed little emotion.

These days, my wonderful children are happy in their lives. After selling the restaurant in Stettler, Kathy now has a government job. George is still working in the hospitality industry, and he is excited to move to Greece to help my sister Cathy run her restaurant. John left the Plaka; he grew tired of the owner continually screwing him over with wages. The checks were continually bouncing. John has been back home in Stettler for a year. He was working at East Side Mario's for a while, but the high gas costs were taking a good portion of his wages, so he quit.

John spends a lot of time with me now that he's back in Stettler. He still smokes weed, but that's it. He's even learned to do his own laundry and pick up after himself. His life has turned around. He has a dream of opening his own pastry shop when we sell the house. George is also a lot freer in his communications with me. All the stress from running the business is gone now, and everyone is able to relax. It's very nice. The time we spend together is now calm, and I treasure it. I now love to spend time with my kids. They have a knack for making me laugh. My sister Cathy is also good at making me laugh. She knows what buttons to push. Her latest thing is teasing me that she's going to marry my son Guy off to a nice Greek girl when he comes to work for her. Even George finds it hilarious.

Cathy wants me to move back to Greece; she's such a dreamer. She reminds me so much of our mother. It makes me love her even more. I laugh and tell her that if I moved to Greece, I'd never sleep again because she never shuts up.

When I traveled to New York, I stayed in Nia Vardalos's hotel from *My Big Fat Greek Wedding*. It's a beautiful hotel but is heavily guarded. I ordered takeaway from a local restaurant one evening, and when the food was delivered, the deliveryman was escorted by security. I loved Chinatown and Little Italy; they were within walking distance of each other.

I saw Trump Tower, Wall Street, and the Dakota where John Lennon was murdered. I went to the site of the Twin Towers with a tour group. It was incredibly moving. The pictures they had on display were heartbreaking.

I visited Liberty Island and Saint Paul's Chapel and watched the emigrant ships pulling into port. I watched *The Phantom of the Opera*—spectacular—and I ate what felt like my body weight in New York hot dogs. John wanted me to buy him a fake Rolex watch, so I went to Harlem. I was accosted by men trying to hawk fake and stolen goods.

I saw where the hit TV shows *Friends* and *Law & Order: Special Victims Unit* were filmed; it was my first time visiting a set. Dogs are treated like kings in New York; they have enormous dog parks where your dog can exercise and socialize with other dogs.

Probably my most memorable trip was the recent one I made to Elvis Presley's house. I spent eight days in Tennessee and explored Graceland, including the grounds and the hangar where his and Lisa Marie's planes were housed. We went to his grave site where he was buried alongside his mother and father. There was another house on the land, which was built after his mother passed away. Elvis didn't want anyone living in his mother's house.

While we were in Memphis, we visited the site where Martin Luther King was assassinated, and we stopped in at Saint Jude Children's Research Hospital to visit the sick children.

Tennessee is a beautiful state with breathtaking scenery. Following this, I headed to Louisiana where I danced on the streets in New Orleans. I caught public transport everywhere and hopped on and off buses wherever I felt like exploring. I thoroughly enjoyed my boat ride through the swamps. It was like nothing I'd ever seen before—lazy alligators sunning themselves on the banks, the old voodoo women of the bayou, the odd gentleman who had a baby alligator as a pet and passed it around for us to hold. Louisiana is a magical place. You can't help but dance. There is live music everywhere. The entire area tingles with life. I loved jambalaya, and lobsters were sold everywhere. I tasted an amazing baked potato and sausage dish that was so delicious I went back the next day for more, only to be told the sausage was actually alligator meat. My stomach did quite a few flip-flops. During the tours of Louisiana, they took us to the area where the wealthy plantation owners lived in the 1800s. The estates were stunning, and by contrast, we saw the slave quarters and cotton fields. It is terrible to think that just a few short years ago, black people were enslaved and treated so appallingly.

My hotel in Memphis was right across Graceland. Every morning at seven, they would start playing his songs. The hotel had a pool there, so one morning, I took my coffee and suntan lotion out to the pool area, sat on a lounge chair, closed my eyes, and just listened to his music. From a young age, I have loved his songs. When touring Graceland, they wouldn't allow you upstairs to the room where he died. All the staircases are lined with guitars, and there is a jungle-themed room as well as a recording studio full of memorabilia. The internal furnishings are the same as they were when he passed away; the carpet has that obvious 1960s look to it. It wasn't a glamorous house, but it *was* a "glamorous" house if you know what I mean. The grounds surrounding Graceland are immense, and the staff required for its upkeep must be quite numerous.

When Johnny and Diane went to Greece, he didn't tell anyone what time he was arriving. My sister Cathy was uneasy about this and wanted to see him right away, so we headed into the harbor early in the morning to wait. It felt like we'd been waiting forever, and we were beginning to feel disheartened when, suddenly, we saw them disembarking the ship. We ran to greet them and then headed off to have breakfast and show them Cathy's hotel where she had a room reserved for them. The first thing John did was strip down to his shorts and run into the ocean. I was so frightened as he went so far out, and I wasn't sure how his strength and endurance were after his previous years of drug abuse. But he was stronger than he looked. He made it safely back to shore.

My nieces took John to a dance studio to learn how to do traditional Greek dancing. Diana went along to learn too. I was so proud when I saw them both dancing and having a wonderful time at the wedding. I'll never forget it.

When George had to attend the baptism of his cousin's son, he was supposed to learn the Greek prayers. He got so caught up visiting with his friends and cousins that he didn't have the time. When the priest asked George to step forward and say the prayer, he was completely bewildered. Aunt Soula stepped up and helped him by whispering the words in his ear.

After the baptism, we headed off to the reception. It was nice to see all the family together again; it hadn't happened since we had lived in Stettler. We took photos of all the Georges together—so many Georges!—and by the end of the night, there were so many drunk dancing Georges! My George was up dancing with Aunt Soula. I'd never seen him Greek dancing before; it was a hoot! My niece Cathy was so drunk she claimed an entire bathroom for herself and told everyone else that they could use the bushes.

In 2012, my stepson George, James and Tergani's son, got married. James, Kathy, and George went to Greece for the wedding. They were all treated very well. My daughter helped where she could, and James' brother John did the cooking. He's an amazing cook, and he caters to all the family functions in Crete. On the day of the wedding, George went to fulfill an old Greek custom known as fill the shoe, where you fill the bride's shoe with cash. George thought he was funny for filling her shoe with Canadian money. One of James' cousins was always playing pranks. He cut his tie, dipped it in eggs, fried it, and offered pieces to the bride's family, who were all eating it! The bride's mother was not happy when she found out, but everyone else thought it was funny.

My stepson, George, works at a hospital in Larissa in the payroll department. He's been working there for over twenty years now. His wife had some health problems; she had a brain tumor. They have a sweet little girl, Christina, who is now five years old. They all came to Canada three years ago. When Christina first saw us, she wouldn't come to us at all, but we didn't care. We were just so happy to see her.

Odds and Ends

Ann and I traveled back to the neighborhood we lived in when Cathy fell from the balcony. Ann was surprised by how beautiful everything now looked. The Spanish people who had taken over it had renovated it, taking inspiration from their heritage. Our favorite bakery had closed down, but the elementary school that Mary and I attended was still there; so was Mount Royal Park where Auntie Mary used to take us to swing.

My niece Electra lives in Missouri. Her husband is named Mike. He is an ex-military and still watches what he eats and what Electra eats too. Electra is now pregnant and hides her chocolate stash from him. My sister Ann is so excited to be a grandmother; she is going to stay with them for three months. She even quit smoking in anticipation.

Uncle Mike's granddaughter Effie, who hated Canada when she first arrived, blossomed into a beautiful young lady. All the boys followed her around town, but she put her head down and learned the language well. She now works with Cathy at banquets for evening weddings, conferences, or meetings. Effie was such a hard worker. When she left Greece, she left behind her first love, Lefteris. She never forgot him but lost contact over the years. My nephew Mike found out where Lefteris lived, and Effie called him up. It was a phone call that resulted in a marriage proposal. Now they're married, and Effie works at the bar that Lefteris owns. They also have two children, Costa and Ilianna. Effie and Lefteris are a lovely couple. They come to visit us in Canada every winter.

Ann and I reminisced over the time I laced my father's orange juice with ex-lax. I didn't tell anyone what I'd done initially. I just sat there smirking, but once it hit, I couldn't keep it to myself. It's known in the family as the best prank ever pulled. No one ever told him I did it; he thought he had a stomach bug.

Mary and I used to stay up late and watch Dracula movies. The house in Pierrefonds we lived in had large windows with trees outside. Mary was so scared she would climb in bed with me. I would torture her by pointing out all the shapes the shadows from the trees were making, which would further scare her.

I've focused a lot on the issues that Jack had, but George was not always an angel either. When he was fifteen, he would wait until James and I were asleep and would steal the family car and go joyriding with his friends. One night, he was caught by the police, and we had to attend the station. George was lucky the police knew his father and were on friendly terms. He was let off with a warning. It put the fear of God into him; he never misbehaved again. I have my suspicions that Kathy was involved in the late-night escapades, but to this day, neither George nor Kathy has confessed.

Yanna

When Johnny injured his arm, we were at the hospital waiting to see a doctor when I met Christina. We became good friends. She told me that if she ever got pregnant, she would let me be godmother when the baby was baptized. Luck was in my favor, and she did get pregnant; it was a beautiful baby girl named Yanna. She had ivory skin and thick dark hair. Christina was a tall lady with a light complexion. After four babies, she had a few extra curves, but she carries them well. I loved Yanna like she was my own child, and so did all my kids; they considered her one of them. As she grew, her hair turned curly. Every chance I got, I would rush to take care of her, change her Pampers, and burp her. Kathy always asked me why she didn't have a sister when she was younger; now she says it is like she does.

I spoiled Yanna whenever I could. I bought her gifts each holiday season, and whenever I went to Greece, I made sure I spent as much time as I could with her. I even brought her to Canada to stay with me for over a year once. She also did so much for me. She took care of me when I was ill. She would clean up around the house, knowing I was a clean freak, and she would cook nutritious meals for me. As she continued to grow, I sent her to stay at Kathy's house because my house was filled with boys, and they would come and go at all hours. It was more structured with Kathy, and it caused a wonderful bond to develop between them. Now they are like sisters and talk on the phone daily. When it was time for Yanna to return to Greece, there were no dry eyes. Her beautiful face was streaked with tears. She was still so much like her mother—elegant even in sorrow. My Kathy was also elegant. She learned it from my sister Cathy. I've never had an elegant bone on my body; coming from the environment I did, I never had the chance or someone to model that behavior to me, although between the ages of sixteen and twenty, I used to get my nails done every Friday and get my hair set and makeup applied. My clothes were always stylish. All that died on the night of my wedding when I didn't receive one sweet word. What was the point? I often wonder what people who got married as a result of love do on their wedding night. Do they lie there and say sweet things? Do they laugh about things that happened? Do they just look at each other?

My aunt Sophie, the beautiful young wife of Uncle Bill, was a hard worker. Uncle Bill worked, too, but was a gambler. He gambled all his money. As kids, he would take us to Blue Bonnet—a horse-racing venue—and he would make us wait in the car while he would go place his bets. When he went home, he acted like nothing had happened. He got away with murder. My auntie hated gambling; she was a saver. Now Uncle Bill had been dead for twenty years, but I still felt guilty about our last conversation where I didn't call him uncle and told him not to cause a fight with his brothers John and Nick. I was his favorite niece, and he just wanted to protect me, and I hurt him.

Life Has a Funny Way

My sister-in-law Toula, whom I met over forty-four years ago, has three children—Angie, George, and Lacy. I was always particularly close with Lacy; she was working with us up in Airdrie for a while but recently had to file for bankruptcy. She had nowhere to go, so she came to live near us with her husband and daughter Athena. Athena asked Kathy to teach her how to mix drinks and work a bar, and as soon as she learned how, she walked out in the middle of the busiest season of the year and returned to Airdrie. Then the trouble with Lacy started. When she did the daytime shifts, she would have her husband sweep and mop the floors. He did the lion's share of the work. Rumors soon started spreading around that Lacy was spending all her time on the VLT while her husband worked. One of the rules of employment is that you are not allowed to gamble during your registered shift. Lacy was never one for following the rules, and it was setting a bad example for the other employees who were quick to throw her under the bus when they were caught.

I made the mistake of offering to loan my brother-in-law some money within their earshot. After that, they were always on my case asking for money. Saki, her husband, was particularly persistent. To get him off my back, I eventually agreed to lend him $2,000. To this day, I have not had a single dollar repaid. Lacy always was a material girl, but I was very disappointed that all the love I had given her was bought and sold for just $2,000. Life has a knack of pulling the rug out from underneath you. Expect the unexpected, they always say.

My brother-in-law Mike was the only one in the family whom I would consider to be well educated. He was able to talk to anyone and was respectful of opinions even if he didn't agree with them. He had never been one to push his thoughts or views onto others. He was also somewhat of a neat freak and would even travel into the village to help clean his brother's house. My brother-in-law John was exceptionally smart; he was also incredibly messy and expected others to clean up after him. And for years, that was what everyone had done. Entire wardrobes worth of clothing had to be discarded in the past due to issues with mold. The mold wasn't John's fault, though; it seemed to be a Greece thing. I had a large suitcase filled with antique blankets handmade by my great-grandmother. Someone sent it to the village; when I opened it, I was so upset since everything was ruined.

CPSIA information can be obtained
at www.ICGtesting.com
Printed in the USA
BVHW031445010819
554891BV00003B/19/P